MW00424055

Secrets of
Ad Agency Owners:
Our Best Marketing Advice

Secrets of
Ad Agency Owners:
Our Best Marketing Advice

Edited by Drew McLellan • River's Bend Publishing

Copyright © 2012
Edited by Drew McLellan

All rights reserved.

River's Bend Publishing
Printed in the United States of America

First Printing November 2012

*We dedicate this book to
everyone who is looking for a better way
to connect with customers
and grow your brand.*

Secrets of
Ad Agency Owners:
Our Best Marketing Advice

Introduction

In 1843 Volney Palmer, the first advertising agency in the US, opened its doors in Philadelphia. Ever since that moment – ad agencies have been dedicated to helping their clients grow their business. In the past 250 years, the tools that agencies have used to sell their client's wares have evolved from a simple print ad in Benjamin Franklin's *Pennsylvania Gazette* to HTML code that follows your web visitors all over the Internet, serving up ads wherever they go.

It's not the tools that matter. What agencies really deliver on a daily basis is smart marketing strategy, a deep understanding of human behavior and motivations and an unflagging desire to help their clients succeed.

As an advertising agency owner myself, I know that my peers – other agency owners spend a great deal of their time guiding clients and offering their best counsel. When you think about it, considering how many different businesses they've worked with over the years – there's probably no one more qualified to give this kind of advice.

Which is why, when I decided to create this book, I reached out to some of the most marketing savvy agency owners I know and asked them to contribute a chapter. I simply asked them to write a chapter that shared their best marketing advice.

What I love about their responses is the wide variety. These agency owners covered the wide range -- from your company's reason for existing to how to take on the Goliath in your industry. What all the chapters have in common is that each piece of advice has been gleaned from years of experience in the field. No theoretical philosophies. Just pragmatic, road-tested truths.

Enjoy learning from these marketing masters. I'm proud to be able to bring their insights to you.

Drew McLellan, *Owner, Agency Management Roundtable*

Table of Contents

The Amazing Power of PR

Roger Halligan, *CEO, H+A International*

Of all the MarCom tools and techniques available to marketing professionals, none is more powerful than public relations (PR).

Regardless of whether you call it "earned media," "free publicity" or "word-of-mouth-advertising", PR (which we believe includes social media) can be one of the most effective methods of creating awareness, influencing behavior and yes – driving sales.

There are many examples and case histories detailing how PR has played a key role in achieving an organizations' goals, and I will share some success stories with you in this chapter. So without further ado, here are two quick examples of the amazing power of PR (relating to the public) that everyone can relate to - "The Oprah effect" and "How social media has changed the world.

The Oprah effect

In this day and age when there is so much pressure to measure the ROI of all marketing efforts, clients are looking for both quantitative and qualitative proof of value. We have a Fortune 50 client who constantly preaches, "If you can't measure it, we can't do it."

If you are looking for one of the best examples of how to measure the Power of PR, look no further than the book recommendations Oprah made on her TV show. She would hold a book up and give it a great recommendation and within days it would sell millions of copies. Sometimes these would be books that had been on the market for many months and were experiencing steadily declining sales, but one word from Oprah and the sales skyrocketed.[1]

Such is the power of a personal recommendation from someone you trust and respect. That is what PR is all about – having someone or something you trust make a personal recommendation or non-paid endorsement. Whether it is a well-known celebrity or a trade magazine, a respected third-person endorsement is one of the most credible and powerful marketing tools there is.

How social media has changed the world

Of course, one of the most influential and trusted sources of information also comes from friends and family – often in that order. You can also include peers in this category, which is one reason social media has become the most trusted form of communications - especially for the Millennials and younger generations.[2]

If you doubt the power of social media (relating to the public) consider how it has helped topple governments throughout the Middle East and fuel social movements worldwide. The protesters in Egypt, Lebanon, and other countries used social media to coordinate their protests, stir emotions, and reinforce their passionate messaging. Likewise, the Occupy Movement mobilized millions of people around the world to leave the comfort of their homes and camp out in cold and damp public parks based on their conviction to effect change.[3]

And the point is?

So what do Oprah and the Occupy Movement have to do with your specific MarCom challenges?

Simply this – your goal is make your target audiences aware of your products or services and influence them to take action. That action is usually to buy your product or service. One of the most effective ways to accomplish this is to have a trusted source influence them to take the desired action. And one of the most effective methods of getting that trusted source to make a recommendation is through PR and social media.

I can provide numerous examples of how innovative PR/Social Media strategies and techniques have been the most critical element in an integrated MarCom campaign. These examples range from product publicity programs that generate seventy-five percent of a company's total media sales leads, to a social media program that sold the majority of tickets to a major entertainment event.

However, since space is limited here, the moral of this chapter is that PR and social media can be your most effective and influential marketing tool when implemented in a strategically creative manner. In addition to being the most credible form of marketing communications, it can also be the most cost effective as there are no expensive media charges for the coverage.

But despite the Amazing power of PR, it is but one of the many tools savvy marketers should implement as part of an integrated MarCom program. The other chapters in the book provide some fascinating insights and examples of other very successful marketing tools and techniques.

Attribution Sources:

1 http://atlantablackstar.com/2012/06/02/publishers-rejoice-oprah-bringing-back-her-book-club/
2 http://h-a-intl.com/?q=node/591
3 http://h-a-intl.com/?q=node/554

Bio:

Roger is the CEO of H+A International, a PR/MarCom agency specializing in B2B corporate marketing and trade show promotion. Prior to launching the company in the mid-1980s, Roger was the Director of Advertising & PR at a Fortune 500 company. He began his career with global advertising and PR agencies.

Stop Talking About Your Product!

Gloria and Nic Wildeman, Founders, Lionfish

Managing perceptions in competitive markets

Question: What kind of agency tells their client to stop talking about their product?

Answer: Not just a good one; a great one.

A 'career decision'?

What a courageous act by the agency strategist! After all, didn't the client hire the agency to do the precise opposite? They *want* the agency to tell *everyone* about their product or service. Right?

Not so much. Transformation occurs when the wants and needs of the *buying customer* are moved into the limelight, in front of the product itself.

Before we dive into the details on that, let's examine how the client and the agency guy get to this point. In all probability, our hypothetical client is passionate and excited about his business, and he wants to enthusiastically share every detail of what went into the making of the product: every line of computer code, every nut and bolt, every quality assurance test. He's proud, and he is overflowing with information.

But here's the problem: the customer is evaluating the product from a completely different point of view. What the buyer wants to know above everything else is: *what will this do for me or my company?* It's certain that high-quality manufacturing and rigorous testing will result in a world-class buggy whip. Yet, if we're trying to convince a trucking company to buy our buggy whip, we'll need to do more than prove a commitment to quality.

Our vignette introduces the first ingredient of an effective brand and marketing strategy: compelling positioning.

A short history of advertising

Dating back to the printing of early newspapers, advertising focused on 'the four P's': Product, Price, Place, and Promotion: what is it, how much does it cost, where can it be purchased, and what clever way can we advertise it? In 1972, a series of articles appeared in Advertising Age magazine that suggested a fifth "P" – Positioning. Reaction was so strong that authors Al Ries and Jack Trout published their seminal book: "Positioning: The Battle for Your Mind."[1]

A lot goes into the process of positioning: market research, segmentation (dividing customers into groups having similar characteristics), and targeting of customers whose needs will be best met by *our* product and *not* the competitor's. In a nutshell: Ries and Trout *put the buyer's needs ahead of the product features and benefits.* They argued that planning for the 'other P's' is only effective once we identify the optimum customers and understand what they care about.

The importance of it all

Research and industry experts agree: American consumers see or hear (or smell!) 3,000 marketing messages per day; a vast increase over forty years ago when the estimate was 500. The advent of digital communication gave advertisers an ever-growing smorgasbord of ways to influence buyers: email, internet ads, social media, mobile advertising just to name a few. Advertising is big business: global ad spend in traditional media for the first 90 days of 2011 was a staggering $26.7 BILLION dollars.[2] That's nearly $296 million per day, or $12 million per hour.

What happens to all of that money and all of those thousands of marketing messages? For the most part: not much. Nobody can pay attention to all of that noise or process it in any memorable way. In fact, our brains are designed to filter out all but the most arresting messages and events. A part of our left brain (Broca's area) has been proven to rank and essentially disregard highly ambiguous or commonplace messages, drawing our conscious attention only to the unusual, most interesting, least common input. Here's an example of how that filtering works: It's unlikely that you'll remember the color of the stoplight closest to your house when you last drove through that intersection, right?

The how of it all

Good marketing consultants have a proven process that leads clients to take control of their message and capitalize on the power of positioning. Everyone has their methods, but here is the 'secret sauce':

Persuasive positioning lives in the hearts and minds of the buyers. Positioning is not something we 'do' to a product or a brand; it is something we do in the minds of the customer.

Audience selectivity is crucial – don't try to appeal to everyone on the planet. Positioning and marketing strategies built around segmented and targeted audiences are what grow business.

Eschew ambiguity. Strong marketing messages are crafted to surround the audience with a confident story that they'll care about – and that moves them emotionally.

Remember: it's not about the product – it's about the customer and what they care about – the 'What's In It For Me.'

Value is the new black. 'Features and benefits' are the supporting actors here. Value-focused language answers the question: "why should I care" – and sells product.

The moral of our story

Clients shouldn't be surprised when their agency surprises them, or even shocks them with a radical recommendation. One of the very reasons to engage an agency is to benefit from a different point of view – ideally from someone who has researched your customer and sees the story through their eyes. If the agency guy is taking your breath away, it's probably a good thing.

Attribution Sources:

1 Al Ries and Jack Trout, *Positioning: The Battle for Your Mind* (New York, NY: McGraw Hill, 2001)
2 The Nielsen Company, State of the Media: Trends in Advertising Spend and Effectiveness, June 2011.

Bios:

Gloria and Nic Wildeman are the founders Lionfish, a brand and marketing firm founded on the quirky notion that the purpose of marketing is to fuel increased sales for business and improved fundraising effectiveness for non-profits. Lionfish focuses on local and global technology, healthcare, entertainment and non-profit organizations. Gloria and Nic count themselves lucky to be surrounded by a team that takes their breath away every day.

Managing relationships is at the core of marketing

Veronica Williams, *President, hmc2*

Businesses of all sizes seem to struggle with how to integrate social media channels into their overall marketing strategy. However, if you reposition how you think of marketing, the role of social media channels starts to become clear. Consider marketing as a systematic approach by which an enterprise can manage individual relationships en masse.

Consider this: A brand is not a logo. A brand is the total experience an individual has with a product or service. In fact, if you've articulated your brand strategy, you have also defined how you anticipate your customer will experience that relationship. If you haven't already done this, it's worth taking the time to at least complete the brand pyramid shown here. It isn't easy, but it is simple.

Key Attributes: Key attributes are often closely related to your vision – they are the values associated with the essence of your brand. Try to articulate that using only four or five key characteristics.

Personality: When a customer interacts with your brand (product or service, staff, customer service and communications), what type of personality will they experience? Again – use only four or five words that describe your brand as if it were a person.

Positioning: What makes you better at providing this product or service than any of your competitors? If you can't say it in one sentence or less, it isn't focused enough. Keep trying.

Promise: When a customer buys your product or service, what problem will be resolved, what do you promise to improve for them?

Even though you've defined the personality of your brand, it is important to remember that an individual cannot have a relationship with your business. A business is an economic unit and as such is incapable of interaction. But people do have relationships with your brand - through you and the people who work for your business, and all the other touch-points involved in the consumption of your product or service.

Your prospects and customers interact with your business through marketing communications, transactions, and customer service. You have already been managing these relationships via a systematic process: through staff training, quality control, customer service, vendor relationships, and marketing communications. Social media are just another tactic through which you can continue to manage a large number of relationships in a nearly real time, proactive and systematic way.

Social media channels are mechanisms that enable your brand to have meaningful engagement with your customers by not only maintaining an outlet through which customers can converse, but also by revealing the authentic character of your organization. When you are developing your social media strategy, don't think of it in terms of sales, or brand awareness, or even ROI - although you should expect to impact at least one of these areas of your business positively through your social media strategy.

Instead, think about how you would like your customer to talk about and experience your products, services, or staff. How would you like them to describe your brand? And how is that different from what they are currently saying? The only way you'll know that is if you employ social media channels as listening devices. Yes, listening is an important part of maintaining a meaningful relationship and social media channels allow you to do this more proactively than ever before.

Once you've taken all these factors into consideration, put it into personal terms – after all, we all have a brand. You manage your personal brand everyday – whether intentionally or not. So, apply the same strategy to your business brand to help attract and engage the right type of prospect.

Questions to consider:

- What type of person would your brand be most attractive to (target audience)?

- Where would your brand be most likely to meet that person (channel selection)?

- What do you think would be an effective way to start a conversation with that type of person (content)?

- How often do you think that person would want to hear from your brand (frequency)?

And, as with human relationships, there needs to be chemistry for the connection to work long term. What does your brand want to get out of the relationship (goal setting)? Why would that person want to continue hearing from your brand (strategic planning)? This is the real "meat" of social media strategy because, lets face it, it's one thing to hook a customer and another to keep them. So the last question needs to be: How will you know your brand's relationships are thriving (measurement)?

Once you've answered these questions, figuring out how to incorporate social media channels into your overall marketing strategy should be relatively simple and should result in more meaningful engagement.

For more on how to develop your brand specifically to this new marketing paradigm, see *StoryBranding: Creating Stand-Out Brands Through the Power of Story* by Jim Singorelli.

For practical tips on how to get more customer engagement through all the digital channels, see *Optimize* by Lee Odden.

BIO:

Big ideas come to life when Veronica Williams joins the conversation. As president of hmc2, she works with her team to develop holistic solutions that build clients' brands and grow their businesses. A graduate from Isenberg School of Management, UMass at Amherst, the AAAA Executive Leadership Institute and the Tuck School of Management's Minority Business Executive Program, Williams has spent the past 20 years working with some of Vermont's best known brands.

If a Tree Falls in the Forest

Lori Jones, *President, Avocet Communications*

As the philosophical riddle asks, "If a tree falls in the forest and no one is around to hear it, does it make a sound?" This is the question Avocet Communications asks before developing any retail, consumer or business-to-business marketing communications program. There is more "noise" that surrounds marketing channels today than ever before. People, including your customers, "turn off" their ability to react to messages and they become silent. So, marketers must break the clutter, and create poignant programs that "make a sound."

Avocet Communications connects this philosophy through the ambitious use of strategy and planning that directs creativity to connect a positive image in the mindset of the customer, while differentiating from the competition and creating customer acquisition. We believe that in order to "make a sound," client insight, agency interplay and teamwork lead to the amazing power of a simple, big idea that branches off and leads to big results. But, that big idea can't take place unless marketers are willing take some risks.

Travelling down a path of least resistance, or what we refer to as the "Sea of Sameness" will deliver some results. The Avocet Communications difference, however, is a disciplined strategic approach of delivering results through motivational, not informational, programs. These marketing thrusts result in increased customer acquisition and excelled sales growth. It is the difference between " maintaining a market" and "defending, capturing and creating markets."

Power Continuity™ is a program that Avocet Communications developed many years ago that eliminates the "Sea of Sameness" with compelling image platforms that increase top-of-mind awareness and increased market share. Continuity, in general, has always been an important hallmark in marketing, but it accomplishes little in actual sales increases. Power Continuity™ integrates memorable images in all marketing venues with strategic messaging that connect brands in the mindset of the customer. Moreover, it sets the stage for long-term marketing strategies

The more relevant the image, the better. However, you cannot forget about strong messaging that reinforces brand touch-points.

When you have the need for a battery, what brand comes to mind first? Likewise, when you have the need for insurance, what company comes to mind first? Energizer's "Bunny" and Aflac's "Duck" are examples of powerful programs that Avocet coins Power Continuity™. The reason these campaigns create huge top-of-mind awareness isn't because of their enormous ad budget, it is the fact that their imagery and message delivery not only differentiates within their vertical category, *but with all advertisers.*

Big O Tires, regional tire and services stores, hired Avocet because of its Power Continuity™ solution. "Little O," a cuddly, little bear with "tire hair" on his head, delivered TV, radio, out-of-home, and in-store messages to Big O Tires female dominated market reinforcing honesty and quality. Within 60 days of launching the initiative, Big O Tires experienced double-digit car count and revenue increases. Arc Thrift Stores also benefited with Avocet's Power Continuity™ program. Arc attributes their double-digit customer count and sale per customer and revenue increases to their multi-media Power Continuity™ campaign.

Power Continuity™ works in B-to-B channels as well. US Electronics, an OEM of remote controls, hired Avocet to ward off the competition through the creation of innovation channels. After researching the competition and speaking with customers, Avocet determined that there was a need for a remote control that could be customized and delivered to the industry within a short timeframe. We strategized brand touch-points and messaging determining that the ability for US Electronics to instantly customize a remote control was similar to fast food chains ability to customize anything someone orders. Avocet developed a national print campaign using a hamburger bun with a remote control covered with condiments and messaging that tied into customization. Along with the print campaign, the sales team set up meetings with potential customers, by inviting them out for a burger and presenting the program touch-points. The US Electronics Power Continuity™ campaign was relatable and compelling. Within one month of the campaign hitting the market, US Electronics had several new customer orders, most notably, a $15,000,000.00 contract from one of the nation's leading cable providers. The right strategy, the right message, the right place, the right time, and the right audience converged creating a program that paid great dividends to US Electronic customers and shareholders.

Many of today's award-winning marketing campaigns may create immediate purchases, but not long-term customers. Customers demand strong value propositions, including low price. Due to the current economic situation, customer loyalty is at an all time low. Power Continuity™ shortens the customer loyalty gap, creating top-of-mind awareness and long-term customers by delivering motivational marketing thrusts. But, only for those advertisers who mitigate the "sea of sameness" and make sure their communications programs "make a sound".

Reference:

"In his book *Purple Cow: Transform Your Business by Being Remarkable*, Seth Godin says that the key to success is to find a way to stand out--to be the purple cow in a field of monochrome Holsteins.

Bio:

With more than twenty years of experience in the marketing field, Lori brings local and national retail, consumer product, business-to-business and non-profit organizations knowledge and experience in all aspects of marketing, advertising, PR, management, digital and community outreach.

A Good Mouse Trap

Amy Hanna Atkinson, *President, RCP Integrated Marketing*

A good website should be similar to a good mousetrap. In this analogy, the mouse is your website visitor (prospective customers), and the trap is your website homepage. We've all seen that putting a cheese-loaded trap in a mouse's path is too great a temptation even for the smartest of mice to resist. And, when they give in to that temptation, and the metal bar snaps down on the little critter, we experience success. Sure, there are new mousetraps on the market that make this activity a little more humane or expeditious, but even the crude, simple models still do the job. And the goal remains the same: trap that little sucker while you have him in your sights and never let him go. The same could be said for technology advances that give us new tricks for converting leads on your website.

But sometimes, keeping it simple is best.

When planning a new website, companies typically concern themselves more with how it looks than looking at it as a sales magnet. Here are some specific questions you can ask yourself to both understand your visitors' needs and place the cheese in areas they cannot resist.

Who is your visitor and what do you know about them?

What are your visitor's needs and how can you help them?

What type of cheese will it take to capture them so that they cannot get away?

To truly capture visitors once you have them on your site, you will need to decide what you want them to do when they arrive on your homepage. Defining these points of conversion (or targeted actions) is key to directing traffic and capturing visitors. Here are some simple examples of points of conversion your homepage can include:

A video

A video is a valuable story-telling tool to expose visitors to your company's people, culture, and explain what you do and why you are different. A video allows for this exploration without risk on behalf of the prospect. This is a soft conversion, but a conversion nonetheless.

A web-only special offer

Rewarding visitors for coming to your website by giving them a web-only special offer is a great way to keep them coming back and gives them something to tell their friends about.

Request a quote or get more information form

In this busy world where each of us have long to-do lists, giving your prospect a simple form where they can fill out their project specifications, questions or desires and send it to you via email, 24-7, allows the visitor to check something off their list … and puts a prospect in your inbox.

Make an appointment

For service-based companies, an appointment is the ultimate conversion when the end result is a sale. Integrating the scheduling page on your website directly with your scheduling software is ideal because it requires less action on the part of the visitor.

Subscribe to our newsletter

Entering their email address to be added to a list for future communications is an ideal opt-in as they are making a choice to continue to hear from you. You can even set your email system (a program like iContact, Constant Contact or Mail Chimp) to deploy a "thank you" note for new subscribers explaining what they can expect from you in the future (a newsletter schedule) and give them other ways that they can connect with you for more frequent information, if they'd like (Facebook or Twitter for example).

"Like" us on Facebook

"Follow us" on Twitter

Subscribe to our blog (RSS)

Subscribing to your blog, liking you on Facebook, or following you on Twitter or your blog are all great ways to continue frequent engagement beyond this initial visit to your site.

Call us

Using a web-only phone number, you can track calls that specifically came from the website.

These points of conversion need to be considered separately from your site's standard navigation (tabs to different pages). And, if you're designing a mobile site or mobile landing page, these could even be the only things that appear unless the visitor chooses to see the entire site. They should all be designed to encourage action from the visitor and keep them engaged with your company.

From a mobile device, conversion becomes even more important as typically a user has a specific action in mind when they search for your site to begin with. Keep the user in mind when choosing the actions you'll make most accessible from your mobile home page. For example, since mobile phones are often used while the user is "on the go", you may be able to assume some of the most popular actions would be to call you or get directions to your location.

Just like any good mousetrap, knowing what's working best will help you plan for the future, as more mice will surely come to visit. Be sure to track your visitors' actions through your site analytics so you can adjust as needed to increase your opportunity for success. Remember, what's working best may have as much to do with the bait as it does with where you have put the trap.

Bio:

Amy Hanna Atkinson is President of RC Productions located in Muskegon, MI. Amy has been with RCP since 1995 and holds a degree in advertising from Michigan State University. As a thought-leader in West Michigan, Amy is often asked to speak about consumer behavior and integrated marketing strategy. In her free time, she enjoys riding her horses and spending time with family and friends.

Do you self-diagnose?

Dan Trzinski, President, Platypus Advertising & Design

I have an analogy for advertisers who want to jump into marketing their goods or services without any strategy or direction. It's like going to the doctor and saying, "I don't feel well. What will it cost to have surgery or write me a prescription without ever diagnosing what ails me?"

In my 25 plus years in the ad agency business, countless clients have come to us asking for help. Invariably, the conversation begins with, "what would it cost to do a television commercial or design a new brochure?" Our response is typically, "are you really sure you need a television commercial or brochure?"

Preliminary research is an invaluable diagnostic tool to use before you go to market, but it's also one of the most overlooked marketing tactics by many advertisers. Most have a whole list of reasons why they want to sell their product, but few have spent the time and effort to learn *why* people might want to buy from them or their competitors. When in doubt, I strongly recommend starting with qualitative research. Qualitative research tests a smaller number of participants, but provides an emotional response to the stimulus. This is critical to effectively identifying target markets and shaping your messaging. In its simplest terms, *who are your customers* and *what will make them buy?*

Qualitative research can take on several forms. It could be:

• Structured or non-structured interviews
• Participant observation
• Focus groups
• In-depth interviews

The qualitative method gives advertisers the opportunity to have real interaction with their customer, to dig deep into specific behavior patterns and to observe actual reactions to a variety of situations. It provides insight into what people do, as opposed to what they may say in a survey.

The biggest objection to conducting qualitative research is the cost. Hiring a professional research firm or marketing agency to conduct qualitative research can be more expensive than developing an online survey or handing out a questionnaire at the time of sale, but it doesn't have to break the bank. Much of the expense is in identifying and recruiting participants. If you are budget-challenged, you need to take on some of that time commitment yourself. Here are a few recruiting secrets to help cut the cost of acquiring participants:

- Offer your own products or services instead of cash for participation incentives.

- If appropriate, get friends, individuals in organizations that you belong to or neighbors to help with recruitment.

- Engage a college marketing class to take on a class project.

- Post notices that you are looking for research participants at neighboring businesses.

- Make a donation to a local church or community organization that will provide you with participants.

These shortcuts could save you thousands of dollars in your research project. They may not be scientifically perfect, but if you have a well thought out screening document, which includes a list of questions that qualify prospects as the proper target audience, you can still get quality information from testing these groups.

The one thing you shouldn't take short cuts with is in enlisting a quality moderator. Look for someone who is experienced in interviewing and observing consumers. Your moderator should also have an understanding about your type of business and your marketing challenges. Taking the time and spending the money to hire the right moderator will directly impact the quality of the testing. The moderator's fee should include writing a report summarizing his or her observations and formulating conclusions regarding the tests.

After the qualitative research is gathered, you may want to test some of those conclusions with quantitative research. Formulating questionnaires or surveys and testing a larger number of participants will allow you to add credibility to the subjective nature of the qualitative data. It will help you project how your theories will play to the masses. These surveys can be done very inexpensively. Online tools, like surveymonkey.com let you build, administer and compile results for under $100.

At this stage, you should have a solid foundation for why people will buy your product or not. In contrast, think of the monetary loss involved in having a campaign that delivers the wrong message via the wrong medium to the wrong audience.

So, before you spend money on your next marketing campaign, ask yourself:

- Do I know who may buy my product?

- What are the triggers that put people in the market for what I sell?

- How does the marketplace view my brand versus others in the category?

- What is the most important perception in the consumer's mind that drives making a choice?

If you don't know, or are unsure about any of the answers, *stop the presses*. You're about to put the lifeblood of your business, the marketing budget, at risk. Spend the time and resources it takes to get the answers you need to move forward. And that usually means investing in some good research up front.

Bio:

Dan Trzinski is a nationally respected multi-media strategist. His agency uses a unique discovery process that helps their clients identify, cultivate and deliver a unique brand presence in the marketplace. It starts with research. Knowledge greatly reduces costly mistakes and makes any campaign that much stronger and most effective.

Get on the Brand Ambassador Wagon—Now

Mike Milligan, *President and Founder, Legato Healthcare Marketing*

A critical and permanent shift is occurring in the way healthcare organizations engage with their patients and employees. In today's socially driven world, both consumers and employees not only share their experiences through word of mouth, many spread their views online, giving them more control and influence over brands—including yours.

A 2011 Global IBM CMO Study revealed that more than 50 percent of chief marketing officers (CMOs) think they are underprepared to manage key market forces–from social media to greater customer collaboration and influence–indicating that they will have to make fundamental changes to traditional methods of brand and product marketing.[1]

This shift in the balance of power from organizations to their patients (and employees) requires new marketing approaches, tools, and skills to remain competitive. Enter: the Brand Awareness Program.

Brand awareness programs can leverage both patient and employee advocates. The key to a successful patient advocate program is to effectively harness the passion of your loyal patients while empowering them to share their views. To help you accomplish this:

- Develop specific program criteria to help you narrow your search for brand ambassadors: Has the person displayed brand loyalty for an extended period of time? Is the person technically savvy? Is he or she respected in the community and professional field?

- Identify potential ambassadors. Do you know individuals who fit the criteria to promote your brand? What about online opportunities? Who is following your hospital on Twitter or liking you on Facebook? Think of other tools you can use to identify candidates to be ambassadors.

- Once ambassadors are onboard, give them a reason to talk. For example, invite them to tour a new addition of your hospital before the general public. When people feel like they're "in the know," they want to share the inside scoop with others.

- Make your loyal patients feel important. When your hospital holds a special event, send ambassadors a VIP invitation with extra tickets to invite their friends. Send a personal note to thank them for their input vs. a canned email. You get the idea.

When developing or enhancing a brand ambassador program, don't forget to leverage your company's most valuable asset: your employees.

Employee ambassador programs are often formed by "cherry picking" a core team to get the brand ball rolling—and keep it rolling. Typically, the team is made up of employees from across the organization, PR, HR, IT, Housekeeping … The common denominator is that all employee advocates have the personality, passion, and knowledge to enhance a brand's image. Many also have a large or targeted network they can tap into to help build customer/patient relationships, reach new markets, generate buzz, and "put a face" on the company.

As you build your employee brand ambassador program, keep these points in mind:

- Advocacy starts at the top. Leaders need to live and breathe the brand. If they do, your employees are much more likely to embrace it. Encourage leadership to consistently communicate about brand and share examples of how they personally bring it to life.

- When choosing a hospital for an overnight stay, 70.8 percent of consumers considered a physician's referral as "Very Important."[2] This shows the importance of building strong physician relationships to help ensure your hospital is top of mind with PCPs and that they act as brand ambassadors for you.

- Communicate. Share key brand messages via emails, newsletters, intranet, voicemails, town halls, and training courses. Employees can't effectively deliver on your brand promise if they don't know what it is or what is expected of them.

- Provide training. Before employees become ambassadors, they need to understand the different marketing messages as well as the services your hospital provides. At the very least, create a list of key messages including an elevator speech.

- Empower employees. Give your brand ambassadors opportunities—not orders. Provide the support and resources they need to successfully represent your brand in both traditional and innovative ways. For example, if your brand promotes community partnerships, consider giving employees opportunities to volunteer in the community on company time.

- Recognize brand advocates. Highlight different ways your brand is being brought to life by standout employees who are effective brand ambassadors. It can encourage individuals to keep up the good work while inspiring other employees to do the same.

The time is ripe for executive-suite discussions on how to better lead—and learn from—your loyal consumers and employee advocates. But before you dive in head first, take a step back and make sure you do your homework. How will you ask loyal consumers and employees to become advocates? How will you monitor your online reputation?

If you can't answer these and other pertinent questions, partner with an agency that has experience developing brand awareness programs.

Sources:

1 http://www-03.ibm.com/press/us/en/pressrelease/35633.wss

2 http://prconline.com/custom/editor/National%20Research/2011%20 PRC%20Consumer%20Guide.pdf

BIO:

Having been vice president of marketing at Prevea Health (Green Bay), and director of communications at Aurora Healthcare (Milwaukee), Mike Milligan has extensive insider knowledge of healthcare marketing. In addition to his healthcare experience, Mike has worked with Fortune 100 companies including 3M Pharmaceuticals, Dow Chemical Company, and Philips Medical Systems.

Do You Have All The Customers You Need?

Craig Barnes, President, Market Growth Accelerators

If you're a business owner or charged with running a business, you know that long-term profitability is dependent on your efforts to:

1. Get more quality customers
2. Keep those customers coming back to buy more
3. Grow your revenues by having customers recommend your product or service to others

Simple, right? You and I know better. It takes a constant effort, everyone within a company doing their part to make it a reality.

I meet small and medium size business owners every week who are struggling to Get, Keep and Grow customers. One of the first questions I ask is: "what is your cost to generate a lead?" This is followed with, "what does it cost you to convert a lead into a sale or customer?" Don't feel badly if you can't answer the questions. You're just like most owner/operators who, if they had heads for every hat they wear, they'd look like a science fiction creation.

The answers to those questions and more are within your transactional and operational data. You just have to pull it out and review the numbers. Here is an exercise you can use that takes the "guess work" out of determining an acceptable "get" budget allocation.

- Define the number of sales/customers you want to make/acquire yearly
- Determine the average lifetime value of a customer
- Establish an acceptable percentage of investment against the lifetime value to acquire a customer
- Calculate the average close or conversion ratio

Once you have those numbers, the formula builds itself. With the permission of one of my clients, here is a real business example that illustrates the process, based on a sales goal of 1,200 new customers to generate $1.9 million in top line revenue:

- Customer Lifetime Value (CLV)= $995
- Acceptable Percentage of Investment (API)= 10%
- Maximum Cost-Per-Acquisition (CPA) = $99.50 (CLV x API)
- Average Close Ratio (ACR)= 50%
- Maximum Cost-Per-Lead = $49.75 (CLV x ACR)
- Leads Required for 1,200 sales @ 50% ACR = 2,400
- Maximum Lead Generation Budget = $119,400

This is a good place to begin, but is just one step in the process. The goal is to not only "get more customers", but also to target the "right kind of customers." To do this, you need to understand what your best customers "look like."

Depending on the size of your business and the amount of customer data on hand, the path to identifying your best customers varies. At the very least, you should be able to review your customer history and determine common characteristics of those who produce the most revenue for the longest period of time. Armed with that information, target your lead generation efforts at those who most look like your best customers. It pays off. Here's an illustration.

Suppose you go to a cocktail party where there are a hundred people. You have one hour to enlist the support of as many people as possible about a cause you are championing. If time is money (remember, you have one hour) then you would want to talk with those most predisposed to your point of view, yes? Sure you would. So imagine if you could walk in and recognize quickly 35 of the 100 who would likely support your cause - you'd want to talk with them first. Same applies to your marketing efforts. Understand what your best customers look like and then spend your time and money talking to them rather than just anyone.

So, what happens when you "Keep More Customers?"

The cost-per-sale is lowered dramatically when your current customers buy more. But, you know that.

Driving more sales from current customers requires building loyalty through exceptional customer service, delivering value and maintaining a productive dialogue with customers.

Does everyone in your company understand that they have a role in keeping your customers? What are you doing to let your customers know how much you appreciate their business … do you have regular contact with them; even if it just to say "hello"?

Customers will buy more if you give them a reason to do so. But, it can't be all about you. Add value to the relationship. Provide them with information and ideas that improves their business.

And, realize that you can "Grow Your Revenues" when customers talk.

The cheapest form of marketing is having your customers recommend your services or products to others. Always has been, and always will be the most efficient sale you'll ever make.

What does your company do to ensure that customers have a reason to tell others about you? How do you measure satisfaction? How do you listen? Do you listen?

Loyalty generates profits. Understanding your customer base and the percentage that are high value, high loyalty is critical to moving others into that group.

Maintain engagement, develop a productive dialogue with customers … that is the key to a profitable relationship.

What's your plan to Get, Keep and Grow Customers?

Bio:

Craig has spent the past 25+ years as the strategic force behind Market Growth Accelerators. He delivers ROI solutions, working one-one-one with business owners or operators to help them:

Get More Customers
Keep More Customers
Grow More Customers

Craig shares his enthusiasm for accelerating customers' revenues in his blog, Boost Your Marketing ROI. http://marketgrowthaccelerators.com/blog/

The most dangerous audience

Megan Devine, Fred Driver, Maureen Dyvig, *Co-founders, d.trio marketing group*

A compilation of stories told by the marketing trio of Maureen Dyvig, Megan Devine and Fred Driver, founding partners of d.trio marketing group, Minneapolis.

Maureen

In College my classes were occasionally led by business professionals. These people were on the front line and told real world stories of how things actually worked. As such, one of my marketing classes was taught by a marketing director for a Fortune 500 food company here in Minneapolis. This company owned, and he was the CMO of, the number two burger franchise in the United States.

One day, our instructor asked, "Do any of you know why number two burger joint doesn't have drive up windows?" (I should note here that this was more than a couple of years ago). I thought to myself, yes, as a matter of fact, I have wondered why they don't have drive ups? He posed the question again, "Think about it, why would they not have drive up windows when the number one burger joint does?"

Space or design constructions? No. Didn't want to spend the money? No. Too late to the game? No.

"The reason," he finally said, "is that I sat in a meeting with eight other marketing executives and emphatically stated, over and over and over again, "People are not that lazy!" You could almost hear him hitting the table with each word for emphasis. People are not that lazy!

Turns out that indeed, people are that lazy. They also have kids in the car, don't want to venture out in the rain, are late or tired or they simply choose the convenience of a drive up window.

Aside from learning that day how much admiration you can gain in a classroom by admitting your mistakes and taking full responsibility, we learned that no matter how smart we think we are, no matter how sure we are of a solution, no matter how much we know our product, customer, market … fill in the blank … we can never, be an audience of one. Costly mistakes have been made with this erroneous assumption. Who knows what may have happened to number two burgers had they been first to market with the drive up window?

I've long forgotten the name of my teacher that day and I'm not sure he would want credit for this story. But I've never forgotten the lesson. I've repeated it to employees, colleagues, bosses, writers, designers, and yes, even a client or two. I've also had to remind myself once or twice. The most dangerous audience in the world is the audience of one.

Megan

Another example of how being an audience of one is dangerous happened twenty years ago when the Mall of America was built. I believed that the Twin Cities area was already saturated with great retail, and that the Mall of America was redundant and would fail. Because I wasn't a shopper, I thought, "I wouldn't go to a mall as a destination, who would?" I was wrong – the Mall of America is celebrating its 20-year anniversary this year and is one of the most successful retail malls in the U.S. As a professional marketer today, I would never let my opinion cloud seeing the value of a business to others.

I've seen many examples of this over the years with well meaning people thinking their opinions are correct when they are not the target audience of a business' product or service. What we are NOT talking about here is knowing your target audience, and crafting relevant copy that feels like you are delivering a personal, one to one message to them. We're talking about being an audience of one – where you let your own opinions influence an idea or a marketing program instead of doing the research to understand what is meaningful to your target audience.

Your own preferences and personal taste help you decide what is best for you, but it's not necessarily in your customer's or prospect's best interest. You have to be able to put yourself in the shoes of the audience you are after, it doesn't really matter what your personal taste and preferences are. Spend time on research, internal and external, and hire someone who can help you determine what matters to your customer or prospect if you're not sure – sometimes you are too close to your own business, product or service. Great marketers can figure out the relevant messaging to a target audience regardless of their own feelings and avoid being the most dangerous audience of one.

Fred

When you are in a position of marketing leadership, it's particularly difficult to suppress your personal feelings, biases and tastes when it comes to developing and judging marketing content. You must fight the urge to impose your will on the process many times in spite of the experience and intuition that has served you well in your career.

A real-world example of not succumbing to "the audience of one" comes from a job I had in college. I worked for a man who owned a single-location, urban clothing store catering to street-fashion conscious inner city young people. The owner was a grizzled, self-taught, pragmatic retailer who was in his sixties and lived in the suburbs. Needless to say, his life experience and perspective was not that of his target audience.

I was continually amazed at the inventory I would see delivered to the store. I couldn't imagine how this guy could gauge the clothing tastes of customers so different than him. When I asked his secret, his answer was simple, "I go to the shows, look at what's out there and if I personally hate it, I buy it for the store." He realized the "audience of one" was his greatest enemy and employed an elegantly simple solution to counteract it.

This is not to say one should ignore one's instincts, but rather to combine them with relevant data from the market and be open to thoughts and direction that may be in conflict with how you perceive the world.

The tiny clothing store mentioned above was a smashing success for over thirty years, illustrating the power of avoiding the most dangerous audience (one).

As marketers, we have accumulated many examples of "the audience of one" over the years. They are mostly fun stories to tell where they never resulted in a marketing program mishap. Fortunately we have more examples of great one-to-one marketing that is successful: when you do the research, understand your market, your customer – their needs and desires – and give them what they're looking for. That's the audience you really want to understand and save the audience of one where it's no longer dangerous – your personal choices.

Steve Tobek for CBS Money Watch has written a blog entitled, 10 Companies With Insanely Bad Marketing where he highlights the audience of one and other marketing missteps, http://tinyurl.com/8la4e8k

Bios:

Megan Devine

A d.trio co-founder, Megan combines broad experience in digital and traditional multi-channel marketing strategies, from creative through analytics in the financial services and retail industries. She brings her expertise to social media through managing LinkedIn's social media group and loves nudging clients to use marketing channels together to build stronger customer relationships.

Fred Driver

Fred is the Y chromosome in d.trio, and one of its founding partners. He brings profound product/services marketing expertise and insights to the table. Afflicted with relentless curiosity, Fred keeps d.trio ahead of the curve. Having toiled in both the client and agency salt mines, Fred brings valuable perspective and boundless creativity to every marketing challenge.

Maureen Dyvig

Maureen plays a vital role at d.trio in the determination of marketing strategy and creative direction for many new and ongoing campaigns. Her experience in multiple marketing disciplines helps her to create well-rounded, results-driven programs. Solving problems and discovering the most creative way to communicate the message is her specialty. Brainstorming is her passion.

Is there really truth in advertising? You bet.

Del Esparza, *President, Esparza Advertising*

Every year, the editors of *Newsweek* run a poll to determine the professions that command the most respect. For the past 10 years, the professions that have topped the list have been firefighters, doctors and teachers (in that order). The ones bringing up the rear are lawyers, advertising executives and car salesman (in that order).

Being a proud advertising executive, I decided to write a strongly worded letter to the editors of Newsweek demanding a recount. Then I went home and watched a little television.

There was a golf club promising to immediately lower your score, a facial cream suggesting that it could make you look ten years younger, and of course, a law firm insisting they could get you money if you'd been injured in an auto accident. Unfortunately, many of the professionals within our industry consistently fail to utilize the single most powerful sales tool in the history of mankind.

The truth.

The truth is – being honest works – especially when it comes to advertising. The best advertising isn't about deceiving. It's about finding the truth of a product or service, and communicating it in a compelling and memorable way. For example, trying on a pair of Nike shoes isn't simply about lacing up a shoe – it's about joining a community of people who believe more about being active, than passive. "Just do it" isn't just the Nike tag line – it represents an honest and motivating reason to purchase products made by Nike.

Honesty is how you should approach every form of advertising you do for your company. But, it is not always easy to determine the honest answer. It includes internal and external research, which will offer clarity in determining true strengths and weaknesses of your product or service. With that groundwork, you can begin to strip away all of their more superficial marketing challenges and discover the real core truth regarding your product or service. In other words, discover the truth about what you are selling, and then leverage the strength of that truth to your customers.

Not all advertising agencies have the capability to discover the core essence of a product or service and unfortunately, not every business has the luxury of hiring an advertising agency to help them identify their core truth. I have a few helpful tips to keep in mind before you spend good money running a radio spot, online placement, television commercial, or any form of media:

- Does my ad clearly communicate the true single most compelling reason to purchase my product/service? Even though it's possible to put lots of information in an ad, your audience only has time (and patience) for one. Pick your number one reason and demonstrate it in a way that cuts through the clutter.

- Does my ad communicate the true emotional reason for engaging in my product/service before attempting to communicate the analytical one? If you fail to first demonstrate how your product/service will benefit your audience, it doesn't matter how much it costs or where it can be purchased. Your prospect wants to believe – help them believe.

- Does my ad communicate the true point of differentiation between my company and my competition? If you can't determine what makes you different – don't expect your customers to be able to make that distinction either. Remember, price, quality and service are not points of differentiation to discuss in an ad. These are attributes that can only be proven to your customers once they've actually engaged in your product/service.

So next time *Newsweek* publishes their survey illustrating the most respectable jobs in America, please remember that the most powerful weapon in the advertising executive's arsenal is the truth. Maybe then *Newsweek* will place us somewhere a little higher on the list.

Bio:

A native of Albuquerque, Del acquired his marketing expertise in a range of fields, from high tech to healthcare. He began his career at IBM, and later advanced to a marketing position with DuPont and Conoco Oil Corporation in Houston, Texas. Del founded Esparza Advertising in 2000.

Four simple truths that make any communications program successful

Jeffrey R. Hoffman, *President & Chief Strategist, The Hoffman Agency*

As an agency owner, I'm often amazed at how many in marketing communications try to clutter our field with buzzwords and catch phrases that suggest only we in the field have the magic keys to success.

Behavioral, contextual, geographic targeting and other current buzz phrases dizzy many marketers almost to a point of stasis. Even branded entertainment is bandied as a new concept – though its roots are in the likes of Milton Berle and the Texaco Star Theater.

Truth be told, the concepts of good communications have changed little since Tarzan grunted at Jane. What has changed is the enormous array of communication channels now available.

But just for a moment forget all the hype, the drama, the Sturm und Drang brought by the acceleration of today's converging marketing options.

The challenge is no longer 'who can I get to buy my product.' Today's challenge is 'whom can I get to pay attention to my product' in hopes he or she will buy.

But even in this environment, there are four simple truths about advertising that don't change. Follow them and you will be successful – whether you use the latest behavioral-contextual algorithms or drop a print ad in the weekly shopper.

Simple Truth Number One:
Real advertising is about creating tangible results.

For most businesses this means increased leads or sales. For non profits, it could be an increase in new members or donors. For others, it could be a significant change in behaviors, i.e. a reduction in water use.

It's easy to get caught up in measuring customer engagement and conversations as the success of a campaign. Those two elements are really intelligence gathering by listening. Again, not a new concept, but true success is based on what you do with that information to create tangible results.

Successful marketing communications programs define the desired result at an acceptable level of ROI and measure against that – a factor often talked about but just as frequently overlooked.

Simple Truth Number Two:
Message is key.

While it is true that media choices help find a targeted market and deliver marketing messages, the message has to be attention getting and relevant enough for its intended audience.

Crafting compelling messages is tough. But it's not magic. It starts with understanding your market and how your product (or service) relates to it. I've seen too many clients attempting to sell products that have no appeal to the intended market and puzzle about why. After watching one client wrestle with what caused sales to increase in a demographic segment he did not target, I asked him what he was learning. His response? The wrong market is buying the product.

That's a breakdown in matching product to target.

The 'father' of the concept of integrated marketing communications, Don E. Schultz, a professor at Northwestern University, says integrated communications "starts with the consumer's wants and needs and works back to the brand."

Without knowing how what you're selling relates to the audience you're selling to, you're just guessing. And well into your marketing effort, you're guessing why people pass you by.

Knowing the product's relevance helps message creators develop messages that are compelling, resonant, and that are actionable.

Getting someone's attention is much easier when you understand what motivates action. Great creative achieves that – even if the only award it wins is getting results. Startling creative without motivation, well, startles.

Simple Truth Number Three:
Go to where your audience is.

This has always been true.

In 1964, Canadian communication theorist Marshall McLuhan put forth the idea that 'the medium is the message' creating a controversy in the advertising world that would rage well past his death in 1980.

In some ways, his theory is tailor-made for this Age of Communications Convergence – especially when it comes to social media and digital marketing.

McLuhan believed that media shapes "the scale and form of human association and action."

In simple terms, he posits that a medium has social implications that reach far beyond content.

Think Twitter. And Facebook. And the Arab Spring.

That's technology contributing to social change.

Newly minted abilities to communicate online with behavioral, contextual, and geographic precision give marketers opportunity to make messages more relevant than ever before.

And it challenges agencies to do their best intellectual work to fully integrate communications across multiple platforms and media types – from traditional to digital – wherever the desired audience may be.

You're after eyeballs and ears, no matter the medium.

Simple Truth Number Four:
Stay the course.

Consistency in marketing efforts pays huge dividends. Digital marketing channels allow for easy and quick campaign adjustments, which often tempt radical change.

Don't do it.

All marketing communications take some time to work. Messages have to percolate in the marketplace in order for the desired action to take place.

Adjusting PPC ads and popular search terms is necessary – but the overall theme and direction of your communications effort should remain the same.

Consistency is how icons are born and results become stronger.

Which truth evaded your last marketing effort? Which did you have to fight for? Did any fade from importance during the campaign? What success did you leave on the table?

Stick to the fundamentals and success will follow – no matter the media path followed.

Resources

Principles of Advertising: A Global Perspective, Monle Lee and Cara Johnson, 1999

Understanding Media: The Extensions of Man; 1st Ed. McGraw Hill, NY; reissued by MIT Press, 1994

Bio:

Jeffrey Hoffman is a 30-year integrated marketing communications veteran with expertise in advertising, public relations, direct response, and digital marketing.

Founded in 1993, his firm has developed branding and marketing communications programs for a variety of national and regional corporations and organizations including several listed on the Fortune 100.

He is a frequent writer and speaker on marketing, branding, social marketing, and behavior change marketing.

Branding: It's About Heartbeat, Not Chest Beat.

Rob Rosenberg, *President, Springboard Brand & Creative Strategy*

During the last decade, there has been tremendous change in the world of marketing and advertising. We've witnessed the explosion of social networks and the acceleration of digital media. Target marketing is now "sushi thin" and customer profiling rivals that of the F.B.I. Yet, amidst all these changes, there is a consistent thread that has remained woven in the fabric of consumer buying. The concept of branding is alive and well and remains at the "heartbeat" of reaching and motivating customers to choose one product or service over another.

That's it - heartbeat! After many years of the industry over-analyzing the concept of branding and numerous textbook definitions, it comes down to this key phrase. And when contrasted with the words "chest beat," used to describe branding's first cousin, "selling," the concept really ticks!

A brand strategy creates an emotional and foundational statement about a product, service, or organization. It creates a promise to the marketplace that places an emphasis on user benefits, not features. And the benefits usually make our hearts beat; whether it's how we feel, dream, hope, perform, or even how others view us as a result of using our favorite brand. All heartbeats. Not chest beats. Perfect examples: Levi's creates a heartbeat with the feeling of freedom and relaxation, not with thread count and fabric data. Coke makes a heartbeat with rejuvenation and refreshment, not the promise of carbonated water, sugar, and caffeine.

Another important trait of branding versus selling is the type of communication that takes place with customers. Today, branding is so engaged in social media and web/mobile interactivity, that it constantly creates an ongoing dialogue with loyalists. Whereas selling is still very much a monologue with buyers, telling them what you want them to hear (aka "chest beat") often in intellectual, factual terms, not emotional ones. Note the key difference in audience interactions: branding engages with loyalists, selling talks to buyers.

Creating a Heartbeat with Internal Audiences

The same distinctions between branding and selling also apply to internal marketing. Since employees are critical to a brand's success - especially in service enterprises - **they have to feel the heartbeat**. There has to be passion in the words they use to describe their organizations to friends, family, and future brand loyalists. Perfect example: Next time you present a new brand campaign to internal stakeholders, don't just inform and educate them (aka chest beat), inspire them! Use sight, sound, and emotion to build a sense of pride and professionalism. Demonstrate how each and every employee contributes to the success of the enterprise and help them understand their role in delivering on the brand promise. Share how their work positively impacts the communities in which they live as well as society as a whole. Studies have indicated that these types of messages and benefits offer real tangible results in terms of employee satisfaction, retention, and customer sales!

Could the concept of branding be this simple? Probably not, but it doesn't have to be obscure and complicated, either. Branding is about creating a heartbeat, inside and outside your organization. Here are a few suggestions to help get you pumped up:

1. **Beat to a different drummer** - your brand has to set your organization apart and provide your products and services with a unique positioning platform. The strategy has to be true and authentic to your organization and tell a story that no other brand can imitate or communicate. Oftentimes, the character of your story resides on the

inside in the very reasons and aspirations that the organization was founded or a product was created. Leadership interviews and a true understanding of the company's vision and heritage are very helpful in identifying the brand platform.

2. **Take the pulse of your market** - your positioning platform and brand promise have to resonate with your key internal and external audiences. Qualitative research has proven to be an excellent methodology for revealing, reviewing, and determining the relevance of brand statements and creative applications.

3. **Reasons to beat (or believe)** – While communicating an emotional story, brands need intellectual and factual support as "reasons to believe." Gatorade demonstrates this balance when it showcases the emotions of victory and endurance, yet supports them with scientific facts based on ingredients and consumer testing.

4. **The beat goes on** - branding is not just a "one and done." Don't check it off your list and move on. Stay with it, both inside and outside your organization. The brand essence must live within the culture of your organization and successful companies use it as a guide for making operational, human resources, and customer service decisions. After all, what good is a brand strategy if it falls apart on the delivery or promise, or employees are not engaged in the story?

5. **Just beat it** - traditional, digital, social...regardless of the media, channels, or vehicles, your brand strategy and creative executions need to be consistent across the board. Important: sync your social media strategy to your brand promise and create standards that speak to the personality and position of your organization (and not the poster). It's amazing how a brand is positioned one way, yet the social media "personality" is completely different.

When compared to selling or other marketing disciplines, branding is about a heartbeat. And when we keep that in the forefront of our thinking and strategy development for both internal and external audience groups, the journey and long-term value of brand building will continue to generate significant returns. And that's an idea worth circulating!

Bio:

Rob Rosenberg is President of Springboard Brand & Creative Strategy, a brand development and communications firm located in the Chicago area. Prior to founding Springboard, Rob was President of a consumer healthcare advertising agency and also a Director of a global pharmaceutical agency. Having worked with over 150 organizations throughout his career, he has been instrumental in the launch of numerous brands and often speaks and writes about the strategies impacting internal and external communications programs. Rob lives in the suburbs of Chicago and enjoys all the restaurants, theater, bike trails, and tourist traps that the city offers.

How to choose the right agency for you.

Jean Whiddon, *Owner, Fixation*

(Or, how to hold on to your agency for longer than the average woman holds on to her favorite pair of jeans.)

A stalwart of the advertising world is the new business pitch. This is when companies looking for an agency pick ones they'd like to "get to know" and invite them to spend days, weeks – even months working on a project. For the agencies, it culminates in a series of presentations - at the end of which one agency will have proved, without a doubt, that it's the best choice for the client's business.

The success of this time-honored practice is reflected in a statistic from a 2012 Bedford Group Consulting survey of businesses that have hired advertising agencies. According to the survey, the length of time on average a client retains an agency is 34 months.

By comparison, a 2010 poll from Consumer Reports' ShopSmart shows the average age of the favorite pair of jeans in a woman's closet is 72 months.

So why do advertising agencies get worn, washed, and donated to Goodwill at a rate twice that of blue jeans? Especially when so much time and effort gets invested in the relationship? Could it be that the relationship was doomed from the start?

There's an axiom in the industry (at least on the agency side):

"The day you win the business is the day you start losing it."

But what if that weren't the case? Wouldn't it be great to know what the client/agency relationship was going to be like before the "I Do's" were exchanged?

Well at the risk of sounding like a bitter divorcee with all the answers, next time you look for an agency consider the following to help ensure the relationship will be long and fruitful:

Have a good think. Determine exactly what you want from an agency – personality, size, skill sets, level of service, rates, etc. – and why you're looking. But don't make it all about what you didn't like about your last agency. Make it about you.

Embrace your culture. If you can define your culture, you've taken a good first step toward finding an agency that will fit within it. If you can't define your culture, you'll risk ending up with a Band-Aid agency: one that quickly eases the pain your last agency caused instead of one that's best suited to your needs.

Weed out the riff-raff. The round 1, pre-pitch questionnaires are valuable. If an agency is serious, they'll respond. If you're serious, the questions asked will be extremely relevant. In answering, if an agency hits on some of the same challenges you experience, it's the sign of a potentially better fit.

Be honest. Agencies appreciate the big picture including where your "pain points" are. You'll get more out of an agency the more you let them in, so start off the relationship with as much transparency as possible.

Is full service too much? Nearly every agency will tell you they're full service. But what does that mean? Print, digital, broadcast, account planning, research, media planning and buying? Define the services you really need from an agency, and get specific.

Better vs. good enough. Some brands need better. Better means more time spent digging through research, providing Nordstrom-level client service, thinking of original ideas, and executing to perfection. For others, good enough is good enough. There are agencies built to deliver each. If you aspire to Nike- or Apple- level success, you want better (and the time and expense that comes with it). If your budgets are tight and marketing efforts are regulation-driven, good enough is for you.

Do some real work together. On paper you've defined the perfect agency/client relationship. Now put it to the test. For those you're serious about, give an assignment – a real one where account, creative and media folks will have to work with you to get the project done. And offer to pay agency rates – it's the only way to see if you get what you think you're paying for.

References. Ask for them. But not just for names and numbers. Come up with criteria for references… and for references that represent, and are willing to share war stories, about a particular need or concern of yours.

A couple thoughts on making the relationship last:

Respect. The agency should assume you know more than they do about your industry. But they know a lot about theirs, too. Remember creative work is open to interpretation, so things are rarely 100 percent right or wrong. If you don't feel an idea is on strategy, explain why and ask for another try. Agencies can be a terrific resource.

Communicate. Just as it's costly to replace employees; similarly, it's costly to replace a tried-and-true agency. Have you been crystal clear about your expectations and given the relationship your best shot? A trusted partner obsesses on your success as much as you do. Don't toss that commitment away before talking things through.

Questions:

- Why are you looking for a (new) marketing firm? And before "divorcing" the current one, are you confident you've given the relationship your best shot at success?

- What's it going to take for a new agency to win you over…beyond the standard, "wow us!"

- When you think about successful, long-lasting relationships in your organization, what do they have in common?

Resources:

1 *Agency Mania: Harnessing the madness of client/agency relationships for high-impact results*; Bruno Gralpois
2 *Crucial Conversations – tools for talking when stakes are high*; Kerry Patterson, Joseph Grenny, Ron McMillan, Al Switzler
3 *Hey, Whipple, Squeeze This: The Classic Guide to Creating Great Ads*; Luke Sullivan
4 *Truth, Lies and Advertising : The Art of Account Planning*; Jon Steel

Bio:

Jean Whiddon is the owner of Fixation, a strategic marketing firm in Bethesda, MD. Clients include trade associations, non-profits and government. A self-proclaimed "accidental business owner," Jean learned business management on the job, relying on a foundation of customer service skills, innate business sense and the advice of others in her Agency Management Roundtable network.

Why Integrated?

By David W. Ralls, *President, air INTEGRATED*

The world of advertising is evolving, with new media and communication channels being introduced regularly. As a major incentive to growth, client brand objectives have shifted from awareness to engagement, customer experience, and driving traffic for the purpose of purchasing. Focus is on relevant and meaningful communications that reach customers at the right time, with the right message. And, most importantly, it's not about reaching just any customers, but specifically those with the highest propensity to buy, share with their friends, and continue to follow what our clients are offering with the intent to re-purchase.

What is Integrated Advertising and why is it more effective?

According to The American Marketing Association, integration is "a planning process designed to assure that all brand contacts received by a customer or prospect for a product, are relevant to that person and consistent over time." The fact is that everyone has fewer resources to allocate these days and the need to have measureable and impactful returns are critical. Gone are the days of integration defined as the combining of online and offline with a common message. Today the opportunity is to integrate strategy, ideas, offers, experiences, using the channels appropriate for that client's customers, and to integrate the timing of messages to help customers and prospects get what they need at various stages of engaging with a brand. For example, when a consumer begins their journey they are often looking for information and as they move into the decision making process they are looking for customer reviews, offers and messages that build their trust. Once they have made an initial purchase they are looking for service, offers on new purchases, reasons to tell others why this brand has surprised and delighted them – in other words, the opportunity to experience being part of that brand's "community" and content they can share with others – things that make them proud to be a customer.

Most clients have a specific objective – for example to drive new sales. With integrated advertising, a consistent message and desired result focus is deployed across all efforts. It makes every resource go farther and work harder. It increases measureable reach and frequency. Case studies show that the integrated approach has proven to be more effective by 2 to 1. Recent Mckinsey research concluded that when companies get "multichanneling" right, they enjoy larger profit margins and yearly revenue growth more than 100 basis points higher than companies that don't. In addition, The Pew Research Center (http://www.pewinternet.org) report shows demographics of user engagement online that illustrate why advertisers need to always integrate their messages, considering all appropriate online and offline channel choices.

Get, Keep, and Grow.

At air INTEGRATED, we work primarily in three focused areas, which we affectionately call Get, Keep and Grow. Our foundation is rooted in intelligence and we use analytics and data analysis to glean the insights we need. As in medicine, we believe that in advertising "prescription before diagnosis is malpractice."

Get is the acquisition of new customers, and not just any new customers. By identifying the characteristics of and creating personas for the high value/high loyal customer, we choose communication strategies, messages and timing to attract and engage the high return on investment customers for our clients.

Keep is about the metric of lifetime value. We all know it is less costly to keep a customer than it is to engage new. In the keep bucket we focus on attrition, re-engagement and loyalty. The goal here is to keep our client's customers coming back over and over and increase the lifetime value of each customer.

Grow is the equivalent of cross sell/up sell. Many clients have multiple products and service lines, each with established loyal customers that have not purchased the products and services of the other departments or divisions. This is an opportunity to co-brand the corporate good name with new or previously un-recognized customer experiences, and sell across customer segments. Launching a new location, division or product, are all good "grow" opportunities, and results are measured in revenue.

Conclusion:

Consumers are engaging across multiple channels and making decisions in multi-dimensional ways. Consumers are savvy, value the opinions of others and want reasons to grow trust in a brand. Both culture and technology influence how people search, make purchasing decisions, and share their experiences. We believe the most effective and efficient way to advertise is to combine appropriate traditional off and online media with the innovations of new media, creating a fully integrated approach. Grow new revenues, increase lifetime value and optimize the cross sell/up sell experience. Nothing feels better than documented success.

Resources:

The American Marketing Association, www.ama.org

The Future of Advertising Will Be Integrated, Mark Suster, April 29, 2011 http://techcrunch.com/2011/04/29

Why Integrated Marketing Works: The Case for Using an Integrated Approach to 21st Century Communications. White paper, May 2011, Integrated Marketingworks, 260 Newport Center Drive, Newport Beach, CA 92660.

Bio:

In addition to his passion for the pursuit of excellence in business, David Ralls prioritizes his family and community. He and Deborah are the proud parents of two amazing boys, William and Jackson, and are also extremely active in the community. David holds an MBA from the W. P. Carey School of Business at Arizona State University.

"Watch out for the competition" (and other ridiculous notions)

Jim Huebner, President, HuebnerPetersen Marketing Communications

"The competitor to be feared is one who never bothers about you at all, but goes on making his own business better all the time." —Henry Ford

I recently made up a new word.

The reason I know it's an original word is because I "googled" it (which is ANOTHER word that was new not too long ago), and it said my "search did not match any documents." So if it didn't show up on 4.99 billion web pages, then I think I'm okay calling it my own original word.

So what's my new word? "Transappleformation."

The real beauty of making up an entirely new word is that I get to make up the definition, too. So here it is:

noun
Trans-app-le-for-ma-tion
[trans-app-ul-fer-mey-shuhn]

1. the act or process of transforming a brand into Apple-like stature

2. the state of being transformed into Apple-like stature

3. change in form, appearance, nature or character in a manner similar to the ways of Apple

Why did I feel the need for a new word? Because I constantly find myself in discussions with clients and staff about approaching brand building "like Apple does." I think maybe it's because—if you haven't noticed—that Apple really doesn't compete...with anyone. And guess what? When there's growing demand for your products and you don't compete with anyone, you can charge what you want, make the profits you want, and rack up the biggest market cap in the history of the NASDAQ (and the NYSE for that matter)...and all that during the worst economic conditions in recent history. So why WOULDN'T a company want some "transappleformation" in their brand?

This whole concept of putting your brand in a situation where you don't really have competition was first introduced to me in Trout & Ries' classic marketing book Positioning. They called it "cherchez le creneau." It's a French marketing expression that says "look for the hole." Basically, Trout & Ries said if everyone else is zigging, you need to zag. You need to go against the grain. Find what no one else is doing and do it. Find your "creneau."

More recently, branding guru David Aaker's book Brand Relevance— Making Competitors Irrelevant certainly refines the point. He contends that marketing's role should not be focused on the expensive and over-sold task of creating brand preference. Instead, it should be focused on creating new "categories" or "subcategories" for your brand. He describes the four vital tasks necessary for creating brand relevance: concept generation, concept evaluation, creating barriers to the competition, and actively defining and managing the new category or subcategories. Diligently performing these four tasks will result in direct separation of your brand from competing brands, making them virtually irrelevant.

The primary appeal to this approach is the profit opportunity it creates. With irrelevant competition comes immediate and significant pricing power. (Again—think Apple!) As long as your brand continues along the path of new category creation, others will simply copy and sell at lesser prices. And while they're busy minimizing profits, your brand remains well on its way to creating the next category and continuing to maximize your profits in the process.

So these are great concepts, but are there any companies actually doing this outside of Apple? Absolutely. Consider how each of these brands have stepped away from "business as usual" and receive more buzz, more attention, and improved company value as a result:

Subway—made fast food healthy
Zappos— new way to buy shoes
Twitter—new method of communicating
Southwest—new way to fly
Starbucks—new way to experience coffee
Tom's shoes—new way to buy and benefit someone else in the process
Pampers—became a parenting resource vs just selling diapers
Facebook—new method of socializing and staying connected to friends

Nearly every brand could use some transappleformation. If yours is one of those brands— and you'd like to explore creating new categories that will make your competitors irrelevant—here are two questions you can ask yourself to help get things started:

• What do we hate about our products as well as our competitors' products? Make a list of actions you could take to address your "hatred."

• What is something no one else in our industry is doing? Make a list of five unmet needs that currently exist in your marketplace.

Bio:

Jim Huebner is President of HuebnerPetersen Marketing Communications. The firm was established in 1989 and specializes in helping make companies heroes to their distribution chains through strategic brand positioning, integrated marketing, and front lines marketing services.

Challenger Brand Marketing 101

John Gumas, *President, GUMAS*

Challenger Brands are companies of any size or industry that are either being outspent by larger competitors, are new to an industry, compete in large or cluttered markets, or for any reason, find that their current marketing resources are not enough to generate the results they seek.

Every industry is loaded with Challenger Brands that are trying to compete directly against larger, financially stronger or more established brands. Many of these Challenger Brands actually have superior products, provide exceptional solutions, and offer a more cost effective alternative than their larger competitors. But at the end of the day, if a Challenger Brand does not have the right messaging strategy and can't get this message in front of the right target audience in a way that is credible and believable, chances are they will fail.

Just because you are up against larger competitors, it does not mean that you can't be extremely effective at marketing. The typical mistake most Challenger Brands make is that they develop traditional marketing strategies. Traditional marketing strategies are tried and true, but they only work if you have the marketing budgets to sustain these programs at a high level over a long period of time.

The key is to think and act like a Challenger Brand. By virtue of circumstances, Challenger Brands have to approach everything they do from a different perspective. They have to throw out the thinking that comes with traditional marketing strategies they have learned and start to think differently. Think of the classic story of David and Goliath. How did David defeat the powerful Goliath? Did he stand toe-to-toe with him? No.

David discovered Goliath's weaknesses and understood his strengths, and then engaged Goliath on his own turf and on his own terms.

The following are five of the most basic mindsets that we believe all Challenger Brands must embrace:

1. **Think and act differently**

   To get noticed and break through the clutter, Challenger Brands need to draw attention to their message and say things that are unique to them. However, it is critically important that you know with 100 percent certainty that your message is relevant to your target audience. The key is to be different and attention grabbing, yet extremely relevant to the needs of the target. Be careful to not be a "focus group of one." Just because you think your message may be relevant to your audience, it doesn't always mean it is. The final judges are your customers and prospects, so be sure you have taken the time to confirm the relevance of your message with your audience. Challenger Brands can't afford to guess.

2. **Own a niche**

   You must identify a niche within your market that you can truly call your own and just as important, you can defend from any competitor moving forward. Challenger Brands can't afford to be everything to everyone, so they must become something very special to a targeted group. What is it that you do better or differently than anyone else in your space? Is this position relevant and important to your customers and prospects? Discover your unique niche, then own it and defend it.

3. **Understand the limitations of your budget**

   Most Challenger Brands play only in those arenas where they have the best chance to win. Don't think about the perfect marketing program because chances are you can't afford to execute it. Instead, think about your total marketing budget and how to create a program that will optimize your strengths and maximize the ROI on the resources you have available. Consider segmenting your target audience into smaller, easier to reach vertical markets or reducing the geographic focus of your target. Your objective is to put yourself in a position to be noticed, make an impact, and win.

4. **Never compete head-to-head with larger competitors**

Challenger Brands understand that if they go head-to-head with competitors that have significantly larger marketing budgets, greater marketing resources, a larger sales force, or better known brand names, using the same strategies will only result in getting lost in the clutter. Develop your own strategy that plays to your strengths.

5. **Become famous for something**

All of this leads up to one, very critical objective for all Challenger Brands – become famous for something. You can never be known or remembered for everything, but you can certainly be famous for one thing. Whatever it is that you ultimately become famous for, remember that it must be unique, memorable, ownable and most important, relevant to your target audience.

Bio:

John Gumas is President of GUMAS, a full service branding, advertising and interactive agency that specializes in Challenger Brand Marketing. John is recognized as one of the country's foremost authorities on Challenger Brand Marketing and is the author of the popular book "Marketing Smart" which details how Challenger Brands must develop marketing strategies to effectively take on their larger competitors.

Can you train yourself to be more creative?

Linda Anderson, *Co-Founder and Managing Partner,*
The Anderson Group

How do "creative types" come up with all their ideas? Is creative problem solving an ability you either have or don't? Can you really train yourself to be more creative?

Some people are more idea-inclined than others, but it's a mistake to think creative skills just come naturally. Even the best strategists, writers and creative directors—people paid to deliver fresh thinking every day—get distracted, stressed and stumped. Here are a few methods to break through those barriers:

Pick your "best brain."

Our brains are amazingly efficient, enabling us to focus on a specific issue or multitask. However, creative problem solving involves four kinds of "thinking" which are done better separately than together: 1) Analytical thinking defines the problem; 2) Conceptual thinking generates ideas; 3) Critical thinking narrows the possibilities; and 4) Rational thinking develops actions. When confronted with a challenge, it's easy to apply the wrong kind of thinking at the wrong time. Imagine a writer trying to define his topic, write content, and edit his work all at the same time! If you're feeling stuck or unsatisfied, chances are you're trying to move too fast or combine too many thinking styles at once. Relax, and pick your "best brain."

The problem is the problem.

Think about a challenge you're facing right now and write it down in a single sentence. It's hard, isn't it? But the truth is creativity feeds on definition, structure and limitation. Many times people mistake "problems" for "situations" that block ideas. For instance, "Our sales are slipping!" is a situation, not a defined problem. "How will we sell more of our most profitable widgets?" is closer, but still vague. "How do we show busy moms that our most profitable widgets save time and aggravation?" This level of definition provides structure while triggering images and sensations that fuel creative thinking.

Answers already exist.

Michelangelo reportedly said, "In every block of marble, I see a statue as plain as though it stood before me, shaped and perfect in attitude and action. I have only to hew away the rough walls that imprison the lovely apparition, to reveal it to the other eyes as mine see it." Was he just being modest? Or was he sharing a simple truth: If you aren't convinced the answer you need exists, you won't find it, no matter how hard you look. Also, mentally and emotionally, the creative process is much easier and more engaging.

Let your mind wander.

In her book, *Writing the Natural Way*, Gabriele Lusser Rico presents a clustering technique to overcome writer's block. It's based on the notion that what we lack is not ideas but a direct way of getting in touch with them. Many times we get stuck because we think we should know where to start, instead of leaving ourselves open to whatever emerges. Thoughts, images and sensations—when given free rein—seem to come in clusters of associations.

To create a cluster, start with a word or phrase, circled, and placed in the middle of a fresh sheet of paper. Then you simply let go and begin to flow with any connections that come into your head. When something new and different hits you, begin again at the center and radiate outward until all associations are exhausted. This technique helps you capture those associations as they take shape, and it also allows you to find surprising new patterns, connections and insights.

Sound familiar?

Analogies and metaphors also are great ways to "see" problems and "reveal" answers. How does your problem remind you of a picture, animal or story you heard about last week? Or, why is your problem like a tomato, a computer or losing weight? This may seem a little foolish, but the principle is sound. You won't find out-of-the-box answers while you're trapped in the box.

Challenge conventional thinking.

Lastly, one of my personal favorites is to take some statement presumed to be true and try to make it false—not to be rude, but to acknowledge that sometimes the best answers are found opposite of where you thought they might. Go ahead, grab a notebook, and set your phone alarm to ring in five minutes. Ask yourself, how are dogs and cats the same? A sampling from my list of 40+ answers below:

Animals
Pets/companions
Four legs
Need food and water
Likes treats
Lap water
Full of personality
Enjoy attention
Make me feel needed
Hairy
Can be petted
Have whiskers
Can attract fleas
Have sharp teeth
Communicate nonverbally
Can be naughty
Poke noses into bags
Not easily forgotten

Want to learn more?

You truly can improve your creative skills! Here are a few of my favorite books—enjoy!

- *A Whack on the Side of the Head*, Roger von Oech
- *Grow*, Jim Stengel
- *Imagine: How Creativity Works*, Jonah Lehrer

Bio:

Biography: Linda Anderson is co-founder and managing partner of The Anderson Group, where she helps companies achieve profitable and sustainable growth by unleashing the power of their brands.

Leadership from operations: Reimagining some key positions.

Glenn Towle, *Principal and COO, Merrick Towle Communications*

Why is a Chief Operations Officer contributing to a book of marketing advice? Because those brilliant ideas in other chapters will be more easily implemented, more effective, and more productive if company leaders have built a top-tier operations team. Typically, marketing communications firms are founded and run by talented, entrepreneurial people. They come from a multitude of disciplines: Account Service, Creative, Media, Public Relations. It's rare to find small to mid-size agencies with someone from the operations team (such as Accounting, Project Management, or IT) in a senior leadership role.

These operations functions are acknowledged as necessary, but too often treated as something for which the expense is to be minimized. "Overhead" it's called - don't want to spend more than is needed to get by. The result? Recruiting for operations is task-oriented, seeking specialists who execute limited duties accurately for the lowest reasonable cost. Meanwhile, those talented, entrepreneurial agency executives keep much of the responsibility for implementing their vision in their own hands. This may work for a while, but tight control has its pitfalls.

As demands from throughout the company grow, leaders are increasingly burdened with day-to-day management duties, leaving less time for their true passion. An unfortunate consequence can be constriction on growth and harried, overburdened owners. This can even escalate to the point of crisis – financially or culturally for the firm, as well as professionally and personally for the owner.

Perceiving operations as a valuable source of leadership is an excellent way for principals of marketing communications firms to lighten their personal burden and increase the entire company's effectiveness. Based on over 20 years of directing agency operations, here are just a few suggestions:

- Rather than hiring a bookkeeper, hire a businessperson – someone with the technical skills to perform the accounting function plus the aptitude and aspiration to run a business. Empower him or her to participate in every facet of the company, developing deep understanding of processes, resources, and expected outcomes. This person's financial reporting will become a source of insight and recommendations, not merely numbers to be passed along to others. It's remarkable what the right person in this position can accomplish!

- Project management is an important role in creative firms of any size. In fact, I've always believed it to be among the most important functions. Done well, it requires seeing beyond budget parameters and allocation of hours; it integrates all agency resources in a coordinated effort to meet and exceed client needs, profitably. An empowered leader in this position not only keeps day-to-day issues off the principal's desk, but facilitates effective decision making throughout the company.

- With marketing firms almost completely reliant on digital tools today, information technology positions are becoming mandatory in ever-smaller organizations. This function can be sub-contracted with some success, but doing so may be a disservice. Having an internal IT resource fully knowledgeable of agency products and services helps ensure technology systems are well designed for current needs and future growth. Even more important, that person can research, recommend, and implement the ever-evolving tools the communication industry is adopting so rapidly, helping keep your firm current and relevant. The leader in this position should be a progressive thinker as passionate about communications as he or she is about technology.

Properly conceived, each of these roles offers considerable opportunity for leadership within your firm. Properly filled, each position relieves burden from agency principals and expands opportunities the company can pursue. Don't fall victim to the restrictive mindset of personal authority and tight control. Rather, embrace the potential resulting from staffing every position in your firm with the best and brightest, even those positions you may have perceived more as necessary expenses than as potential leaders. Don't let increasing management burdens distract you from your passion. Instead, enjoy the benefits of delegating responsibility and the personal reward that comes from spending time developing the people you surround yourself with.

When recruiting, do you find it challenging to get the whole picture of a candidate through the interview process, as I do? Try using an objective assessment from Strategic Talent Management (strategictalentmanagement.com). An STM evaluation adds invaluable depth of understanding of a candidate's potential fit in the role and your organization.

Wonder how to keep these operational leaders (and everyone on your team) empowered, engaged, and motivated? *Start by reading Drive*, by Daniel Pink. This book offers insights that will affect how you recruit and lead your team.

For more of my thoughts on leadership, operations, management, staffing, change and growth, read my blog at momentumagencyadvisors. com/blog/

Bio:

Glenn Towle, Principal and COO of Merrick Towle Communications and founder of Momentum Agency Management Advisors focuses on internally developing the senior leadership team and externally consulting with principals of other marketing communication firms on company culture, operations and change.

Making a Profit by Pretending You Can't

Kurt Kleidon, *Vice President and General Manager.*
Kleidon & Associates

Go to any marketing awards ceremony and you are sure to see it, sitting there like a thoroughbred perched on a pedestal: The fantastic nonprofit project, best in show award already presumed and patiently waiting for a chance to trot a victory lap. The design is original and on target, and the headlines read like a cool breeze on a summer day.

Then there is the for-profit business piece, respectable in its own right with above average design and nice photography. But the closer you look, the more you notice a disturbing flood of unnecessary company details. Finally, there it is, the classic tagline-by-committee: "Experience the (your company name here) difference." Consider your marketing ship sunk.

Why do nonprofit marketing campaigns succeed when so many traditional businesses chase their own tails? Many nonprofit organizations matter to people, directly and immediately. If they produce something ineffectual, someone that they serve may very well die.

Well, not really. But at least nonprofits usually believe that this could be an outcome, and that is the point. How would you market your company if you knew that a mediocre campaign would let a person's life expire?

For starters, stop spending money on marketing crap (MC). MC is the advertisements, websites, brochures, Facebook posts, etc. created because it seemed like a good idea at the time. MC is anything dumped on the intern's desk because you were too cheap to hire a professional. MC is anything decided by committee. MC are projects started in a different decade than they are finished.

Marketing is about standing out; making yourself memorable. The adage for doing this is "show, don't tell." If your taglines simply tell people that your company is different, then it probably isn't. The more you push an unoriginal description--faster, cheaper, smarter--the less likely it is that anyone will believe you.

At some point in every campaign I reach the point where I tell the client that we need to define their company's differentiator. This can be difficult, especially for organizations that have hung their principles on the same hook for decades. It takes critical thinking. It takes creativity. And it takes the ability to change.

Nonprofits have a built-in advantage in defining a difference. Often fueled by grant money, nonprofits can be assured that a direct competitor is unlikely to come along and steal market share. The Grand Canyon National Park, a nonprofit organization, can rest peacefully knowing that a competing national park is not going to pop up down the road. Sure, nonprofits still need to compete for grant money, but chances are that they have already found a way to stand out.

The big question is how to begin thinking about your company as if it were a nonprofit. Your competition is real, as is your overhead. We can't pretend that these challenges don't exist. What you can do is adjust your brand perception with marketing that goes outside of the expected message for your industry. If your competitors all tout decades of experience, become the hip, new kid on the block. If your industry is steeped in tradition and seriousness, crack a joke. Get noticed. Think outside the ad.

Nonprofits rely upon the belief that they do good work for people. Embrace that philosophy in your business as well. Whether you sell a service or a product, your staff, your brand, and your messaging should all align under a theme with this conclusion: What you provide is important. If you believe it then other people will, too; and when other people believe your service or product is important, the sale is a friendly, easier process.

(I'm sure it is needless to mention that if you can't convince yourself that what your business provides is important, get out of it. But I'll mention it anyway.)

If you have already done all of the above, reconsider the methods by which you are reaching potential customers. Nonprofits often have great success with public relations. Harnessing the power of the media can be one of the most effective and cost efficient ways of getting in front of new customers. An ongoing public relations plan is the ideal way to start, but simply sending out a press release when you have news to share can also create interest in your company.

Whatever your mission or your method, connecting your company to a higher goal can breathe new life into it and into your marketing. Let your inner nonprofit guide the way to actual profit.

Resources:

Mashable.com: The site covers everything from PR to pop culture. If you can connect the dots between the crazy ideas from the site and the innovative ones, you might just find a new niche.

Ragan.com: This site recommends marketing tips as much as it suggests things not to do. There is something to be said for keeping yourself out of trouble.

Ask yourself these questions:

• Can you weed out your current Marketing Crap to make room for real marketing?

• Have you ever compared your impression of your company's brand with a third-party evaluation of the brand?

Bio:

Kurt Kleidon is the vice president and general manager of Kleidon & Associates, one of the longest standing, full-service marketing firms in the

Akron/Cleveland market. He specializes in creative and strategic marketing and public relation campaigns for organizations in the fields of tourism, hospitality, professional services, economic development, shelter, and industry. And, of course, he has worked with many nonprofits. Contact him with questions or thoughts at kurtk@kleidon.com.

Who likes the logo?

Michelle Nelson, *Owner, Tap Communications Inc.*

How process is the key to logo approval

As anyone with experience in logo design will tell you, a board or committee discussing a logo can be like a pride of lions closing in on a newborn gazelle. A logo in its infancy – that is, at its early concept stages – is a delicate thing. It hasn't had the opportunity to develop all the brand attachments that make it robust against criticism or, worse yet, suggestions for improvement, and yet it is often unfairly expected to already be "the Nike swoosh".

Tap Communications has more than 20 years' experience presenting our delicate logo offspring to committees, boards, and city councils. We know the pain. To our credit, we also learned over the years, and especially in the last five years, how to achieve the desired outcome with very high approval rates.

Here's how we do it.

It's all about managing expectations, long before any pencil ever hits paper. Make sure the key people you're working with on the client side understand that logo development is a process, not a magical unveiling of "the perfect logo." You need to explain, and to repeat often, the difference between a brand and a logo and that attaching all the meaning you want the logo to symbolize takes years of consistent messaging.

We go to great lengths to point out that our job is to create a symbol which, over time, can have the right connotations easily attached to it. Once we feel that principle is understood, we then proceed to a process we call "jumpstart," which is a series of individual interviews involving everyone who is going to vote on acceptance of the logo. For the sake of discussion, let's use a board scenario.

Before we set up the interviews with the board, we find out more about them. Who are the opinion leaders? Are there any issues? Knowing the board dynamics can go a long way in preventing surprises and better preparing us for the presentation of the logo. This process gives everyone the satisfaction that they were consulted and had input; it also gives us the opportunity to manage their expectations and help them to understand the process. All the comments are compiled in a Board Interview Report which essentially becomes the rationale for our creative concepts. We then make a formal presentation to the Board, where we reiterate our key principles of logo development and the process we are following.

Once we have acceptance of the Board Interview Report, we then develop the initial concepts. We undergo a rigorous culling process internally before presenting our best ideas to the client. Clients need to know this; it's reassuring. When we present these logo sketches, we present them in a black and white pencil sketch, on presentation boards. Presenting them in a PowerPoint makes them seem less substantial and too easy to dismiss.

The presentation to the Board of the four or five pencil sketches is the first of two meetings. Before we show them anything, we tell them they are not making any final decision, but rather providing us with input so we can narrow down the logo development to one or two of the most promising ideas. We then say we are going to show them the concepts quickly (i.e. about three seconds per logo), and then ask them to vote for their favorite in a secret ballot. We immediately count the ballots and present the results. That is the point at which they can offer comments, rather than before. Note that we do not want to engage in any type of focus group testing, which we strongly feel is not appropriate for appraisal of creative concepts.

At the final meeting with the Board, we present our recommendation. We find that Board members are interested in seeing how an initial pencil sketch has been refined. If they liked it before, they will like it even more now. We also then go on to present our colour recommendations and to show applications of the logo, such as on a t-shirt, or signage, or on business card. Showing the recommended logo in actual usage goes a long way to engendering acceptance. It becomes "real." We also remind them of the Board Interview Report and the brand qualities that, over time, we want the logo to represent.

In summary, you can gain logo acceptance if you emphasize that it is a process, not a popularity contest; that you are the logo experts and know what you're doing; and that you involve the board in the process through the presentation of initial sketches at one meeting and final approval at another. In the end, it is the confidence in this process and your professional ability that they are voting for, even more than the actual logo design itself.

Resources:

Kellogg on Branding Alice M. Tybout and Tim Calkins, eds. John Wiley & Sons

Place Branding Robert Govers and Frank Go Plagrave MacMillan

Why we hate pre-testing http://www.rethinkcanada.com/rethink-news/opinion/2010-11-02/

Why we love pre-testing http://www.rethinkcanada.com/rethink-news/opinion/2010-11-16/

Thought-Provoking Questions:

- Do the decision-makers share my differentiation between "brand" and "logo"?

- Has everyone, including our agency team, bought into the process we will follow?

Bio:

The owner of Tap Communications Inc. in Saskatoon, Saskatchewan, Michelle Nelson has led numerous strategic planning and branding initiatives for clients with multiple stakeholders. Michelle holds a business degree from the University of Saskatchewan.

What is your Partnership Plan?

Christine Madsen, *President, Mad 4 Marketing, Inc.*

Create connections with partners that touch your target audience to multiply your marketing outreach.

Even though businesses associate advertising agencies with "creative," and while creative is obviously vital, I can say after 20 years as an agency owner that it's equally important — if not more important — to create partnerships for our clients.

Whether your company is focused on serving consumers or businesses, you need impactful name recognition in the community. When it comes time to get in touch with your target audience, you want that foundation of trust at your fingertips. But these resources don't pop up overnight. They need to be researched, initiated and nurtured. Even the most stable of connections or networks need your energy and attention in order to stay fresh and relevant. Personally, I believe that the time and effort it takes to cultivate and keep those relationships is invaluable.

My agency becomes intimately involved in our clients' business strategies. We develop or refine branding platforms, link creative with brand positioning, prepare marketing budgets, and manage deliverables. Even in our digital world, reputation and word of mouth heavily influence those spenders and decision makers. Therefore, that partnership remains a hefty factor when it comes to our marketing plan for each and every business.

So how do we go about developing the most effective Partnership Plan for our clients? It starts with analyzing the existing Partnership Gap by going over questions like these:

1. Who doesn't know about you but should?

2. Who has a negative perception of your company or its products?

3. Who do you believe has the most synergistic businesses to yours?

4. Which community leaders, local celebrities, or sports figures could easily relate to your business or products?

5. How about nonprofits? Do you have a passion that relates closely to your business or product offerings?

One example of how we apply this Plan is when one of our health care clients wanted to expand into a new county. They faced different competition and had less name recognition than in their home region. Through our extensive connections in the new county, we showed them how to integrate with the local community and meet many of its key players. We also helped them create effective sponsorships with local companies. This not only ensured better name recognition and streamlined communication to the potential customer base, it created a reciprocal feeling of goodwill and drove new patients to their doors.

Another example is when a government agency wanted to provide commuters with a monetary incentive. They needed a financial partner to help facilitate gift cards that fit some unusual criteria and large quantities. Through our connections, we were able to develop a program and secure the tools for them to exceed their new-commuter customer goals.

We also optimize synergies between our clients whenever possible. A local college asked us to promote a new marine engineering program, so we connected them with our marina management client. This allowed the college to have access to the marina, and their accompanying shipyards, for a day-long photo shoot, providing the school with enough images to produce several collateral pieces in addition to a trade show booth and a new website. The college saved money by avoiding stock photography fees and permit fees, and it did not waste time searching for venues.

Another time we aligned a major music company with politicians who had a passion for the arts. This partnership made the politicians more aware of the importance of music education (benefits to reasoning and math skills, etc.) so they could support or sponsor bills regarding funding of music/arts education programs. The positive exposure led to increased sales of the music company's products for years to come.

What about clients who have governmental or regulatory constraints? When asked by a local governmental entity to coordinate an extensive employer outreach program to large corporations, we were able to pick up the phone and get our client in the door without a hassle. And even on a smaller, grassroots scale, we were able to open many corporate doors for a casual food restaurant franchisee who wanted additional exposure for his lunch menus and catering business by bringing tasting samples and promotional materials to local businesses. This increased lunch traffic and catering orders in a short time.

What's the key to sustainable and strong partnerships? Exploring and developing liaisons that can develop into mutually beneficial relationships. By understanding a client's business plan and assessing their Partnership Gaps, an ad agency can begin building a successful Partnership Plan— and a sustainable partnership that benefits both sides.

Bio:

Chris has always stayed true to her Partnership Plan philosophy. She long ago realized there is a reason networking is not called net-eating or net-sitting. Lining up the right people for opportunities has served her well and gained her leadership positions within dozens of community and business organizations over the years.

How to Build a Stronger Brand Image through Public Relations

Nancy Marshall, President, NMC

The most successful brands hold a powerfully positive position within our psyche. They live in our hearts and minds. How do they get there? Through stories, images, and relationships. In my career as a PR professional, I have told thousands of stories, shared thousands of images, and even built thousands of relationships to build successful brands.

My earliest experience with storytelling for brand building was while working in the communications department at Maine's Sugarloaf Ski Resort in the 80s. A retired pilot named Paul Schipper was skiing every single day that Sugarloaf was open, year after year after year. At one point we realized he had a streak going, like Cal Ripken. We started putting press releases out…first to local media and then to larger and larger media. Every 100 days that Paul skied, we would stage a celebration, whether it was a parade on the slopes, a party, or a visit from a state official.

The media loved Paul's story because it entailed an ordinary man doing an extraordinary thing. He wasn't a great skier, but he sure was tenacious. Once, he went out at midnight because he had to drive to Poughkeepsie, New York the next day for his son's graduation from culinary school. Another time, after 20 years of this streak, he was diagnosed with cancer and his doctor wanted to perform surgery immediately. He postponed until summer, because he didn't want to end his skiing streak.

Our PR efforts landed stories in the *Boston Globe*, *USA Today*, *People Magazine* (twice) and "Good Morning America" (they sent their crew up to

Sugarloaf and did a live shot to open their show). Paul became known as "the Iron Man of skiing," and his streak garnered more media coverage for Sugarloaf than anything the resort has done in more than 55 years.

The PR campaign that evolved from "Schipper's Streak" had the full support of the ski area's management team. As a PR practitioner, nothing makes my job easier than a management team that understands the value of establishing a cohesive, consistent, and unique brand identity that accurately portrays what the company has to offer its customers. Whether you are competing on a local or global scale, having a great product is no longer enough. There are lots of great products. Because there are so many products to choose from, customers' expectations are higher.

We are constantly bombarded with promotional messages, so it's much harder than ever before to capture the customer's attention. You can no longer sit back and wait for customers to come to you. You have to establish a distinctive identity – like a thumbprint – in the minds of your customers. Find what is unique and different about what you have to offer – something your customers will relate to – and then use it to set yourself apart from the competition. Creating a successful brand doesn't have to cost hundreds of thousands of dollars. Targeted public relations, an important component of brand-building, is cost effective and has proven to be a very effective means of generating excitement about our clients' identities.

The integrated approach to brand building – including advertising, marketing, public relations, and now the superstar, social media - are all part of building a strong and sustainable brand. When all these tactics are used together, you can hit your target market from all angles. Public relations help the public understand a company and its products. PR allows you to tell your story in a thorough and authentic way. It helps a company achieve 'transparency,' which is what customers demand in today's economy. Working to generate positive media coverage is a big part of public relations. Stories in the media are like third-party testimonials, and people are more likely to believe what they read in a news story than in an advertisement.

With social media, we can now engage in an ongoing dialogue with fans and followers, sharing thoughts, ideas, photos, and videos. In our work with the Maine Office of Tourism, we have been able to build a community of enthusiastic Mainers and people who love Maine but live elsewhere. Every day, our online community shares photos on Pinterest, answers trivia questions on Facebook, and tweets stories that are picked up by the media.

There's nothing more exciting for me than working with a client to build their brand in an integrated and strategic way, and then setting their brand free so it can grow and flourish in the hearts and minds of their customers. All the while, we tend to the brand as a gardener would tend to his or her crops, making sure the crops grow and deliver a healthy harvest of positive marketing results each year.

Questions:

- Have you performed a brand audit on your own business?

- When you think of marketing, do you only think of what you pay to put out there in the media?

Resources:

The Fall of Advertising and the Rise of PR by Al Ries and Laura Ries

UnMarketing: Stop Marketing and Start Engaging by Scott Stratten

BIO

Nancy Marshall feels lucky to have discovered her passion for public relations at an early age. She started doing PR in Maine right out of college and founded her agency, NMC (Nancy Marshall Communications) at age 31. Her agency is now the best-known public relations and integrated marketing communications business in Maine where she proudly lives with her husband and business partner, Jay, and their two sons who are avid ski racers.

The Secret to Our Successes

Tom and Ty Robinson, *Robinson and Associates*

For the past four decades, at Robinson & Associates, we've helped to build one of the largest financial institutions in Mississippi, now ranked in the top 50 in America ...

For the past three decades, we have helped the nation's largest quick service restaurant franchise grow its business in Mississippi exponentially ...

For the past two decades, we have been an integral member of the market team of one of the nation's leading metal building manufacturers, aiding in the marketing of tens of thousands of buildings from churches to schools to manufacturing and warehousing operations to community buildings such as gymnasiums and fire stations ...

For the past decade, we have worked to help reverse the negative trend of high school dropouts, encouraged under-skilled workers to seek retraining and prompted downsized workers to take advantage of available educational opportunities ...

And, the secret to our successes is **RELATIONSHIP**!

Every day we serve as the marketing arm of our clients, doing those skills that they are not staffed to do, bringing that important outside perspective from a creative yet practical point of view. We write effective and actionable marketing plans, create and produce award-winning advertising materials, outline the marketing strategy and design the graphic elements for websites and emerging media opportunities, support public relations and crisis management efforts, are recognized for our media buying acumen, and create memory-making events.

Equally important, we are team players who like to involve our clients in the creative process. And we are competent business people who have the financial strength to do the job with no impediments.

It's the relationship we establish with our clients that allow us to continue to do top quality work for them.

The Golden Rule applies not only to clients but suppliers as well. We all work as a team to meet and exceed the goals of our clients. We get better work out of our suppliers who are treated as partners rather than vendors.

When our clients call our office, they know that they will be heard. We do not believe in automated answering systems. We do have voice mail, but when our phone rings, a live person answers the phone – and, it could be anyone from the receptionist to the president. We don't have Caller ID – we answer regardless. Every call is important. Every call has potential. And, every call should be treated as if it has potential.

Because of the relationships we've established, there are employees of some clients who believe we're fellow employees who work in their marketing department. We're already top-of-mind when a project comes up.

We know how to work within a budget. We're commended for the amount of work we can do with limited funds. And, the reward for a job well done is the opportunity for more work!

We don't have problems … we have solutions. When a client calls, it may be job-related or it may not. "I'm calling you because I don't know who else to call" is the best compliment we receive, and we do our best to deliver. We're known for having answers.

We are Robinson & Associates, Inc., working with a simple philosophy of judging our success by our clients' successes.

Bio:

Father-son team Tom and Ty Robinson and their seven seasoned marketing professionals lead a small, textbook classic advertising agency with an impressive array of national and regional clients. While their manners are stereotypically Southern, their methods reap national recognition and profitable rewards for their clients and their agency.

To do great work... make a difference

Joseph Romanelli, President, Romanelli Communcations

"Wait, so you're saying even if we choose you, and decide we want to spend our money with you, you still might not work with us?"

This is an actual statement from a potential client during an agency pitch. My answer was an unequivocal "yes, we may turn you down."

You see, it's been three years since we invoked a new slogan, mantra and guiding principle for our agency. Namely, "Building Brands We Believe In." This means, we will only work with you if you can convince us that you are more than just another business trying to honor the almighty dollar. If your sole purpose for going to work is to push another, unnecessary widget to another, unknowing consumer, we'd just as soon you take your business elsewhere.

It was three years ago, while sipping on a cold Saranac Pale Ale (a client) in our third floor conference room/bar/photos studio affectionately known as First Draft, that my creative director Bernie Freytag hit me with this idea. Wouldn't it be great if we only worked with the clients we love working with and jettison all the ones that don't really fit with our approach? Easy answer, of course it would be great. At least until we go out of business.

But after a couple more pints, we began to hatch an idea that might just be sustainable. The reason that focusing on Brands We Believe In might be a viable strategy is that we actually do our best work when we are truly inspired by a client. Let's face it, every agency has those clients that they love working on. That they get excited telling everyone, "Yes, indeed, they are our client. Oh, and that great work you see, We made that!"

As Jason Fried and David Heinemeier Hansson posed it in *Reworked*, to do great work, you need to feel that you're making a difference. That you're putting a dent in the universe. That you're part of something meaningful.

The second reason this strategy has been successful is that clients want to feel like their agency "gets" them. There's nothing better than presenting a powerful idea to a client and seeing their eyes light up because the creative team has found a way to describe their business in a way they never could quite articulate to customers.

The Agency/Client Relationship is just that, a relationship. What makes a great agency/client relationship is the same as what makes a great relationship between two people. This is at the core of our approach to finding and Building Brands We Believe In. There are plenty of reasons to get into a relationship ranging from the benign lustful physical attraction to deep-rooted feelings of trust. But more important than all of that, and perhaps more important than love, is the feeling that you truly believe in someone. Without that belief, a relationship is doomed to fail.

By focusing on values, we were able to better empower employees. We acknowledged that everyone wanted to be part of something bigger and aligned our agency's values with those of our employees. As David Casullo points out in *Leading the High Energy Culture*, it is only through this acknowledgement of employee truths, we are able recognize our organization's truths.

So what are we looking for in a brand? Does it have to be some non-profit that's feeding the poor in Africa? Can a simple product become a brand that an agency can believe in?

The answers here are actually quite simple. Here's our litmus test for a brand that inspires us...The Brand

1. Is about more than financial success
2. Is one we can grow with
3. Wants to make the world a better place

Great brands have always stood for more than just profits.

Nike's #1 goal is to Serve the Athlete and inspire people to participate in sports. Just Do It!

Starbucks is about more than a $3 cup of coffee. It is a third place. In 1981, Howard Schultz (president and CEO) first walked into a Starbucks store. A year later, in 1983, Howard traveled to Italy and became captivated with Italian coffee bars and the romance of the coffee experience. He had a vision to bring the Italian coffeehouse tradition back to the United States. A place for conversation and a sense of community. A third place between work and home.

As one Harley Davidson executive stated, What we sell is the ability for a 43-year-old accountant to dress in black leather, ride through small towns and have people be afraid of him."

Certainly it is true of many brands that have grown to be great, but it's also true of startups that have the audacity to say this is a problem that needs fixing and maybe I can do something about it. We've witnessed this first hand with small companies that simply choose to say, I'm going to build my business in this crumbling neighborhood because someone has to take a stand. Someone has to make a difference.

So back to that client, who seemed so taken aback at my seemingly arrogant answer telling him that in fact, the decision maker in his RFP is not just him, it was both of us. Well, he told me after he awarded us the job (and we subsequently found they were indeed someone we could be inspired by). He said, "You said you wouldn't work for just anybody. I liked that. You know what, we don't work with just anybody either. Let's build this brand that we both believe In."

Bio:

Joseph Romanelli is President of Romanelli Communications with offices in Clinton, NY and Boston, MA. Joe succeeded his father, Don as President of the company which was founded in 1973. Joe has spoken nationally on social media and marketing for tourism, beer and wine, and other industries. He is a graduate of Union College with a degree in political science and still works with political campaigns and public affairs. In his free time, Joe and his wife Susan enjoy travel, art, food and wine.

Setting the Table

Cliff Callis, *President of Callis & Associates*

When I was growing up, one of the daily chores that my brother, sister and I shared was setting the table for dinner. It was the one meal during the day that the entire family enjoyed together. My mother, who preached good manners, taught each one of us how to set the table correctly. When it was your day to perform, each one of us knew what to expect. We would get the silverware and napkins out and set them up exactly how we were taught. Sometimes we would need a reminder, but most times, it was done right, the first time, and it was done before anyone sat down to eat.

In the advertising agency business, setting the table is paramount to client satisfaction. Whether you are working with a current client or attempting to sell a new prospect, YOU determine if they will be satisfied. Let me explain. I've always believed that when I am providing professional services, I am the person that is responsible for making people happy, and the way you do that, is by establishing early on what the expectation is. My mother let us know that her expectation was that the table be set in time for dinner. When that was accomplished, she was happy and we were happy (because she was appreciative). If you want to make someone happy, find out what they expect and determine whether or not you can meet or exceed it. Know for sure that you can. Think through the process that you will go through to get the work done. Understand what can go wrong. Expect the unexpected. Talk it through with your co-workers.

Never accept work if you can't meet the expectation, regardless of how bad you want or need the work. You're just asking for a problem and eliminating any hope of establishing a long term, mutually beneficial relationship. If you're working with a client, communicate their expectation back to them and establish clearly in their minds what you are going to do to meet their expectation, how long it will take and how much it will cost. This is typically done in writing with a proposal or project authorization of some kind but the message should also be delivered verbally, face to face if possible. This enables you to read body language and make sure that your message has been delivered and understood.

You have just set the table.

Now it's up to you to deliver. How do you do that? By doing what you said you would do, in the time you said you would and by charging the amount you said you would charge. Sounds easy, doesn't it? It is, but there's more to it than that. Most times, there are things you can't control. Someone doesn't perform as expected. Other projects get in the way. The creative process takes longer than planned. There's a production glitch. Although you can't anticipate exactly what will go wrong, it's a safe bet that something will. So you build in time and budget to handle the unexpected. Consequently, you are still able to deliver on time and on budget because you planned it that way.

Now, if you want to make the client really happy, deliver more than you said you would, sooner than you told them you would and charge them less than what you said you would. How can someone possibly be unsatisfied? They can't, unless they're never satisfied and then you better think about whether you really want to work with them. When you set the table correctly, you put yourself into a position where you under-promise and over-deliver.

Now, when you're in a sales situation with a potential new client, it's easy to promise anything to get the job. I've seen lots of salespeople do it over the years. They want the sale. They want the work. This is the last thing you want to do. Make sure that you understand the expectations first. Understand what it is going to take to make the prospect happy. Be specific. Ask lots of questions. Talk about process. Determine goals. Answer questions directly and never lie. Don't even stretch the truth. Be honest, open and straightforward. Let the prospect know that things don't always go the way you hope they will go. Things happen. Things change.

There may be a problem you both will have to deal with. When you set the table, you will start to build credibility and you will build the foundation for a successful project and an ongoing relationship.

So, how do you set the table with your customers?

How could you make more sales by setting the table?

Resources:

ecallis.com
Callistetics ecallis.com/blog

Bio:

Cliff Callis is founder and President of Callis, an integrated marketing agency founded in 1987. Cliff grew up in the retail business and graduated from Missouri Valley College. Callis provides marketing, advertising, public relations and digital media services to clients in outdoor sports, energy, and a variety of other industries.

The No Problem Solution

Dan Duval, CEO, McDougall & Duval

A few years ago, I had a "moving" experience that forever changed how I insist my company does business…and revealed something you should keep in mind when selecting a marketing firm.

My family and I were moving into a new house, and since the days of bribing our friends with pizza and beer to help us move were in the past, we started looking for professional movers.

Initially, we found a reasonably priced company, but things turned ugly awfully fast. As we were trying to finalize the details, the crew chief exhibited a terrible attitude. Anytime I asked a question, he seemed bothered. If I made minor requests, he would instantly say "no."

Not only did he not value me as a client, he seemed to barely respect me as an individual. Yet somehow, when I fired him to hire another moving company, he was surprised.

By comparison, the replacement movers had a much better attitude. In fact, the foreman kept using one phrase over-and-over. Every question I asked or request I made was met with "No problem!" It wasn't lip service to keep the client quiet. He had a sincere desire to make my move appear seamless, regardless of whatever was going on behind the scenes.

They delivered a tremendous experience that, when I thought about it, could be applied to my own company's work as a marketing firm. Not only would we look for vendors who shared the "no problem" approach, but that instantly became the standard for how we deal with our clients. They've got enough to deal with on a daily basis, so when they hand a project to us or ask a question, they shouldn't get any pushback. We just have to deliver. No problem.

As managers and business owners, we often hear about the importance of finding the right "fit" for potential employees. "The Right Fit" has been the subject of academic studies, and articles in every business publication.

Even Steve Jobs, in the March 7, 2008 issue of *Fortune*, acknowledged that good recruiting is "ultimately based on your gut. How do I feel about this person? What are they like when they're challenged? Why are they here?"

Matching your business with the right vendor requires the same chemistry, especially when you're talking about your marketing firm. After all, you are entrusting your brand to them, so they need to be more than a vendor.

Instead of just pitching clever creative, their proposed campaigns should meet your strategic goals. The firm should understand – and act – like a partner in your business's success, and you ought to have 100 percent confidence that they'll do whatever it takes to help you thrive.

Of course, saying "no problem" can be an empty promise unless the agency has the skills and expertise to deliver on whatever requests come up. If a marketing firm is going to make that pledge to all its clients, its team needs to be as flexible and adaptive as yours.

Many agencies rely solely on their expertise in a particular industry and become known as specialists in that area. Yet in his article "All Hail the Generalist" for the *Harvard Business Review*'s blog (June 4, 2012), Yale lecturer Vikram Mansharamani explains why "a collection of specialists creates a less flexible labor force." The crux of his argument is that the more someone works within a particular field, the more likely they'll exhibit an "ideological reliance" that limits their potential.

"The closer you are to the material, the more likely you are to believe it," he explains. "In more straightforward language, a man with a hammer is more likely to see nails than one without a hammer."

In an increasingly uncertain and interconnected business environment, that ideological reliance can limit the creative thinking and problem solving skills of specialists.

On the other hand, he writes, "there appears to be reasonable and robust data suggesting that generalists are better at navigating uncertainty."

His analysis supports something we've all seen as the rate of change has increased in technology and the workplace. If your company is going to take advantage of new business horizons, your team – both internal and external – needs to be flexible and adaptive.

Succeeding in the interconnected business world of today means having generalists working on your behalf. They are the ones who can take your request, respond "no problem," and then figure out a way to make it happen.

At the end of the day, if you're looking for a new marketing firm, remember the "no problem" solution. First, the ideal agency should be a strategic partner focused on your success, rather than their own. Second, make sure they have the capabilities and personnel that will allow them to deliver on their promises.

Focusing on those points will make your move go smoothly.

Suggested References:

Forbes, March 7, 2008

Harvard Business Review's blog: http://blogs.hbr.org/

Bio:

After several years working as a copywriter for some of Boston's largest ad agencies, Dan Duval and his wife, Bonnie, opened an ad agency in a small one-room office at the Plum Island Airport in Newburyport, MA. Today, McDougall & Duval is home to 12 full-time employees. The agency has won numerous national and regional awards. Dan resides in Newburyport and has an 11 year-old daughter named Maddie.

Inspire your customer: Use words that sing.

Susan Armstrong, *Armstrong Chamberlin*

As a writer, I continually marvel at the power of words.

Many of the world's greatest love stories began with beautiful letters, brimming with emotions that captured the imagination – and the heart – of their beloved. Likewise, the bitter words of anger have poisoned more than one relationship, resulting in family feuds that span generations.

Passionate proclamations have inspired entire nations to change the course of history. When Martin Luther King declared, "I have a dream," millions of Americans began to dream with him. And, in September of 1962, President John Fitzgerald Kennedy rallied support for the space program by telling his fellow Americans, "We choose to go to the moon… not because it is easy, but because it is hard." Imagine! Convincing people to do something because it is difficult.

We respond because — in our heart of hearts — we all want to be motivated to take an action. The right words, the right rhythm, the right tone and voice…together these finely crafted messages propel us forward. The same principles should be applied in a well-crafted marketing message.

In our agency, we have a simple creative philosophy. Our writers are encouraged to abide by two rules:

Rule #1: Always remember you cannot bore anyone into taking an action.

Rule #2: Powerful ads make the reader or viewer feel something.

When either of these rules is violated, the copy falls short of its goal. The ad must engage the reader and connect with her in an emotional way. It has to evoke a strong feeling that results in a desired reaction. This could be a smile or a tear, or the dawning of comprehension. Whatever the reaction, it must lead to the next step in the buying cycle.

Ask any advertising writer why he loves his job and he will tell you, "It feels so good when you get it right." Ask him why he hates his job and he will respond: "It's really hard to get it right."

The inherent challenge in writing great advertising copy lies in making sure the ad tells the right story in a way that connects with the intended audience. It isn't enough to make people laugh, or cry, or jump for joy – if they don't remember the name of the product you are selling.

When our more experienced writers hit upon this magic combination, they can barely contain their joy. They are eager to share the concept with the account team, and look forward to seeing the final execution. They literally wait with bated breath to see whether the client recognizes the gift we bring. And, when the client accepts the ad, a tingle of excitement runs through the entire agency. Why? Because we know it will work, and we can't wait to celebrate.

Likewise, when the idea is good – but not great – our team recognizes there is still room for improvement. The writer will present her idea at a creative meeting and wait for the response. For many years, our creative director would take these "mostly good" ideas and hand them back to the writer with a single question: "Is this the best you can do?" And, our finest writers always, always, admitted they would like an opportunity to try a little harder.

We have a simple description of these "line drive" ads as well – the ideas that come close, but don't make it to "home run" status. In our company, the creative director is likely to read the concept carefully before handing it back to the writer. "It's nice copy," he will say, "but it doesn't sing."

I have no idea where this phrase originated. Was it in a book somewhere that David Ogilvy wrote? Does it refer to a beautiful bird that looks lovely but has no voice? Is it a reference to a poem that has all the right words, but evokes no real emotion? I can only tell you that it is the phrase that best describes those ideas we can't accept for our clients.

This copy-that-sings goal is a lofty one, rarely captured without supreme effort. But I would encourage you to strive for it. Insist upon it. Your product deserves no less.

Bio:

Susan Armstrong is President and CEO of Armstrong Chamberlin, a strategic marketing agency in Wichita, KS. An agency owner for more than 30 years, Susan has also taught business marketing and advertising copywriting. She believes the right business story will capture the consumer's interest, and engage them in the buying process.

What CMOs Want

Elaine E. Ralls, Ph.D., Chief Executive Officer, air INTEGRATED

It was 1998. David, my business partner and I were planning – how could we make a difference in the advertising world? What about our agency would set us apart? How could we grow a business that was a game changer for clients and an agency that had a meaningful differentiation?

We decided to take the time honored approach to the possibility. Gap analysis. What would CMOs recognize as the defining criteria for partnership in the changing environment of advertising agencies? To find out, we conducted our own research with CMOs across America. The input was consistent and telling.

It was easy to see what CMOs didn't want, and surprising to see how they defined meaningful differentiation. What they didn't want fell into administrative categories, which we quickly learned had more strategic value than we had realized. Most of these CMOs were from large organizations where processes are "buttoned up." They expected their agency partners to have the same respect for and prioritization of, business processes. Some examples of where there were concerns with agency relationships include being "nickel and dimed for minor services," inaccuracies in billing, inability to manage budgets and inconsistencies in account oversight.

What they wanted is what got our attention and fueled our excitement. What CMOs wanted, more than any other attribute in their agency relationship, was intelligence. Their priority was to know their ROI on marketing and advertising. Further, to support this they wanted a way to measure the ROI that was consistent with the metrics that they personally are measured on. Metrics that include revenue growth, the value of acquiring new customers as well as the ROI on retention efforts, the value of promoting new products, services, locations, ideas; what's working and what's not. CMOs want validated confidence that their agency "partner" is watching their dollars, making changes as necessary and getting the most out of every resource dedicated to marketing and advertising. They want concrete information to take into the board room to validate their budgets, underscore their successes and show rationale for recommended changes.

So, our job was clearly defined then and is the same now. Lead an agency that takes an "intelligent" approach to budget allocation, implement effective campaigns and produce objective and insightful reports. Now, a good many years later, our foundation of analytics + ideas = results (air) has supported our clients in good times and bad, and has resulted in long term, high confidence relationships with many of our signature clients. Our vision is "Ideas that create change," and our campaigns prioritize measureable and meaningful results for the client.

Although the tools we have to work with today have changed significantly, input from corporate America is not that much different than it was then. There continues to be a thirst for knowing what's working and what's not, as well as a need for presenting the results in objective ways that allow for continuous learning and improvement. Frustrations remain in all service businesses for missed deadlines, inaccuracies, lack of efficient processes and the like, so having Integrity as a core value and "doing what you say you will do" cannot be understated. Building trust in today's business world is about integrity.

Analytics in Advertising

At air INTEGRATED, our approach to "intelligence in advertising" has at its core our foundation in analytics. Our "Cyclone™" (the cycling and cloning of your customer data) system is based on marketing technologies that allow us to analyze, predict, segment, and glean important insights for advertising that customer data reveals. Data-driven insights influence our creativity. The result is that we deploy campaigns focused on growing revenues, market share and reputation/loyalty/advocacy.

Although the definition of analytics has evolved over time and certainly means different things to different people, we are not alone in prioritizing analytics as an intelligence engine that helps us produce award-winning creative and integrated strategies.

In 2010, *Forbes* published a special report stating, "In simple terms analytics means using quantitative methods to derive insights from data, and then drawing on those insights to shape business decisions and ultimately improve performance." *Forbes* provides examples showing how both Best Buy and Olive Garden used segmentation and predictive analysis to improve efficiencies and results.

Clearly, the use of sophisticated marketing technologies is being embraced to improve results and grow market share. Don Peppers and Martha Rogers, Ph.D. of 1 to 1 Media say it this way: "Thanks to the evolution of data capture and marketing analytics tools, companies can now analyze and act on a wide range of customer insights… and develop relevant marketing strategies that the competition can't."

Resources:

When CMOs learn to love data, they'll be VIPs in the C-Suite, by Crain Communications. Advertising Age, February 2012.

Why Predictive Analytics is a Game Changer, by Dave Rich and Jeanne Harris. http://forbes.com/2010/04/01/analytics-best-buy-technology-data-companies-10-acce

The Next-Generation Revenue Generation: Strategies for Success, Don Peppers and Judi Hand. 1to1 Executive Dialogue, 2011 Peppers and Rogers Group.

Bio:

Elaine has an MBA from Arizona State University and a PhD from Nova Southeastern University's School of Entrepreneurship. She serves on the board of the Better Business Bureau, is active in Women President's Organization and Vistage, an international organization of CEOs.

17505558R00061

Made in the USA
Charleston, SC
14 February 2013